NESTA MAUDE ASHWORTH, SILVER FISH
AN AUTOBIOGRAPHY

A Guiding Life

Edited by
Mary Ashworth and Margaret Spencer

◆ FriesenPress

Suite 300 - 990 Fort St
Victoria, BC, Canada, V8V 3K2
www.friesenpress.com

ISBN
978-1-4602-7330-2 (Paperback)
978-1-4602-7331-9 (eBook)

1. Biography & Autobiography, Personal Memoirs

Distributed to the trade by The Ingram Book Company

TABLE OF CONTENTS

I shall
pass through
this world
but once.
Any good therefore
that I can do
or any kindness
that I can show
to any
human being
let me do it now.
Let me not defer
or neglect it,
for I
shall not pass
this way again.

PROLOGUE

On July 5, 1974, Nesta Gervaise Maude Ashworth sat up in her hospital bed and said cheerfully, if a little smugly, "You're not supposed to survive your third coronary." But she had done just that. On her release from hospital she was exhorted to take life gently for a while, a distasteful prospect for one who had led a very active life. Relatives and friends, particularly those in Guiding, pleaded with her to write down the stories she had been entertaining them with for many years. She agreed to, and at the age of eighty-one began to write her memoirs.

Nesta Maude was born on August 13, 1893, the youngest of three surviving children of Claudine Ina and Edmund Maude, a biscuit manufacturing executive. She had two older brothers, Alan and Ronald. A year or two after Ronald's birth, Claudine and Edmund suffered the disappointment of a stillborn son. For Edmund a second disappointment occurred when the next baby was a girl. Nesta soon learned that girls were not as important as boys and did not need to have as much money spent on them.

From an early age Nesta challenged this assumption that boys were better than girls. If boys could play hooky from school so could girls — which she did at the age of six! If boys could ride their bicycles recklessly, so could girls. If boys could be scouts, so could girls, and with this challenge she began her life-long service to what was to become, because of her and a few others, the internationally known Girl Guide Association. In her adult life, she continued to challenge the notion of male supremacy. If men could drive tractors and trucks, so could women — and so went the story of her life. When she was a teenager, someone told her father that the name Nesta meant "a lamb." He is reported to have groaned and said, "Was ever a child worse named!"

For the first ten years of her life Nesta lived in Highgate, London. It was always a source of great pride to her that she had been born within the sound of Bow Bells and could therefore call herself a Cockney. London was to remain throughout her life her favourite city, and during the Second World War she gave it outstanding service.

But the first of the three wars that her life was to span was the Boer War, 1899–1902, and it was to watch the volunteer soldiers marching through the streets of London on their way to the docks where they embarked for South Africa that she played hooky from school at the age of six. During the Boer War it was the fashion for children to wear on their coats a button bearing a coloured portrait of one of the generals in the field. Years later Nesta wrote, "Was it a forecast of the future or the attraction of the name that made me select Baden-Powell as my particular idol?" In May of 1900, the town of Mafeking in South Africa, which had been besieged by the Boers for seven months, was relieved by General Robert Baden-Powell who later founded the Boy Scout movement. Nesta recalled the day the news reached London. "I remember so well being taken by my father to watch from a window the celebrations of Mafeking Night, but it certainly never occurred to me that one day I should be shaking hands with my hero."

In 1903, Edmund Maude was told by his doctor that his health was very precarious. If he left London and lived quietly in the country, he might survive for five more years. The family moved to a large house situated in a lovely garden in Crowborough, Sussex. The peaceful surroundings worked wonders. Edmund lived to be eighty-eight, dying in 1944 having been predeceased by his wife who died in 1914.

Nesta longed to attend a large school for girls, but this was denied her as Crowborough was too small to support anything other than small private schools. Alan and Ronald were sent to Rugby, one of England's foremost schools for boys, but Nesta, being a girl, was not given an equivalent opportunity. In 1907, however, she was invited to become the companion to a girl of her own age in a household where money was plentiful. The girls had their own governess, their own ponies and dogs, and they travelled frequently on the continent.

It was during the years between 1907 and 1914 that Nesta became caught up in the Boy Scout movement. She began as a Girl Scout, transferred to the Girl Guides when the Association was officially started, and in 1979 became an honorary Boy Scout when she was inducted into the 81st St. Faith's Troop in Vancouver. At this last enrolment she said with pride, "I have made the Promise three times, twice as a Scout and once as a Guide."

The 1914–1919 War brought new challenges. Nesta was one of the first to work on the land in the newly formed Land Army, but as soon as women were eligible to join the Royal flying Corps, the precursor of the Royal Air Force, they joined the Mechanical Transport Section and drove everything from staff cars to heavy trucks and tenders.

In 1920 she married and spent the next few years raising a family. Tragedy struck in 1929 when her eldest child and only son was found to have severe epilepsy for which there was no cure.

He died in 1942 at the age of twenty-one having spent the last seven years in a home for epileptics. During the 1930s Nesta found time to play an active role in the Girl Guides once more, running a company and carrying out the duties of District Captain.

The Second World War (1939–1945) was for Nesta in some ways a repeat of the first. She and her two daughters were evacuated from their home in London to a farm in Hampshire where once again Nesta worked on the land. Five months later, however, the "phoney war" showed no sign of turning into a real war and fears that London would be bombed were abating. Nesta's elder daughter, Mary, joined the Land Army, and the younger, Margaret, went off to boarding school, leaving Nesta free to return to London. She quickly became a member of the Women's Voluntary Service and drove mobile canteens all over London and outside the capital to areas hard hit by the bombing that followed Hitler's conquest of Europe.

After the war Nesta returned to Guiding, this time to work with physically handicapped Guides. But in the early 1950s she and her daughter Margaret sailed for Canada to join Mary in Vancouver, British Columbia. It was a little while before the British Columbia Girl Guides discovered that they had one of the original Crystal Palace Girl Scouts living in their midst, but once they found her they never let her go. To her delight, she was able to carry on her work with handicapped girls. But when increasing age brought increasing deafness, she gave up her work with the girls and devoted more time to talking to groups of Guides and Guiders about the early days of the movement.

From 1969 on her health slowly declined. Her third heart attack in 1974 was followed by increasingly poor circulation in her right leg, which was amputated in the spring of 1981 after she had suffered considerable pain. She was almost eighty-eight, but when a well-meaning doctor suggested that she should be content to spend the rest of her days in a wheelchair rather than learning to walk on an artificial leg, she retorted, "I intend to walk into my church on two legs" — and fourteen weeks later she did. She died on July 13, 1982, as a result of another severe heart attack. At her request, there were no flowers at her funeral, the money going instead to set up a fund to help handicapped British Columbia Guides go to camp.

The memoirs as they appear here have been edited very little, and then only in the interests of clarification.

CHAPTER I:

Early Days
1900–1907

Nesta begins her story with a vivid recollection of Christmas, 1900, when she was seven. The "bad accident" she refers to later nearly cost her her life at the age of ten. She was riding her bicycle at high speed down Highgate Hill when one wheel got caught in the tram tracks. She flew over the handlebars onto the hard pavement below and was fortunate to escape with only a very badly bruised knee. For this escapade she was banished to the country. Her parents, meanwhile, were planning to move from London to Sussex.

Christmas at the turn of the century for me and my two older brothers began with the train journey from London to Coventry where we always spent two weeks of the holidays with my mother's parents, our dearly loved Grandpa and Grandma, and some of their six sons and grandchildren. Train journeys in those days were always fun, lots of porters, hot water foot warmers for the ladies, and luncheon baskets with exciting things like chicken legs which we were allowed to eat with our fingers - strictly forbidden at home!

It seems to me that winters were colder in those days for there always seemed to be skating on the canal that ran at the bottom of Grandpa's garden. Although I cannot remember being pushed in a little chair, my brothers have told me that they used to toss up for the privilege of *not* having to push "little sister"! On Christmas morning, everyone went to the parish church, the predecessor of the present Cathedral, in which we had all been christened. Grandpa had given the old stone font, and his many descendants were grieved at the decision of the architect of the present structure to relegate it to the crypt. The adults and older grandchildren stayed to Communion and we younger ones walked home feeling very important, knowing that 'Cookie' would have some tasty snacks waiting for the "wee yins."

After lunch came the excitement of presents, given and received. Grandpa's were always handsome bicycles and cameras and Grandma's were useful hair brushes and bedroom slippers. We children, according to our ages, presented our gifts, usually home-made, watching eagerly to see how they were received. I wonder how many cross-stitch kettle holders Grandma received from each age group of grandchildren, and Grandpa's fretwork pipe racks would have filled a museum! I had barely outgrown the category of the youngest grandchild when Grandpa died, and his eldest son took over the big house and Grandma moved to the Dower House. The family gatherings ceased and we all went our separate ways.

I suppose the years that had the greatest influence on my life lay from about 1905 to 1913 — in other words, from age twelve to nineteen. Up to 1905 my education had been, to say the least of it, sketchy! From 1898 to 1902 I attended Byron House in Highgate, a school well ahead of its time and one which was building a good reputation for itself. It was run by the Misses Legge on the "open area" principle (reintroduced in the 1960s as a quite new concept) with all classes taught in one large room. Miss Catherine taught

English, Miss Florence let us draw and paint and learn about nature and music, and with Miss Jessica we jumped and ran and did physical drills and played rounders, and because we all loved Miss Jessie we struggled with our "tables" and tried to make five times four make twenty! Most Byron House girls went on to one of two girls' schools, but luckily I was only at the one selected for me a year, for I hated every minute, and because I was unhappy I learned nothing. A bad accident kept me out of school for some months, and I went to live in the country. I ran wild with a boy cousin from India who was getting ready to start his English schooling.

When I joined my parents again they had left Highgate and bought a house in Crowborough, Sussex, where the only educational establishments for girls were the local National School or a little "Dame" school kept by a German musician and his Scottish wife with an assistant who taught all subjects to about fourteen pupils, some of whom had a slight mental or physical handicap. No records were kept or reports issued, and I had no homework so again I have to admit I learned nothing.

One of my early recollections of Crowborough concerns an old gentleman who was definitely a "character." He must have been at least ninety years old, and every fine afternoon his daughter would settle him on a bench in the centre of the village, and as soon as school was out the old man would start spinning his yarns to any children who came to listen. I often stopped by for the tales were well worth hearing. You see, old Paynter had been a real smuggler, one of the young lads who had led a string of ponies from the coves and inlets on the Sussex coast to the hiding places inland. He also claimed to have led one of the packs of ponies laden with flour which had been ground in the New Mill at Crowborough and which was destined for London to be used in Queen Victoria's wedding cake. I have sometimes wondered in later years if some of the tales we heard were really stories the old man had learned from his father and attached to himself—but no matter. He was a colourful old character and dearly loved by the small fry of the village.

Another old gentleman, also a Crowborough resident, was generally referred to as a recluse, and when I asked my mother what a recluse was she said "a hermit." As the only hermits I had read about lived in caves and depended on charity for their daily food, I found it difficult to associate this life with a large and very well kept house and grounds which I passed every day on my way to school, and I longed for an opportunity to meet the hermit. It came one day when my mother gave me a bundle of handbills about a jumble sale for the church, with instructions to leave one at every house I passed on my way home from school. At the hermit's house I did more than push the leaflet through the letter box; I rang the bell. The door was opened by a nice motherly housekeeper, but while I was explaining my errand, a voice demanded to know who was there. The housekeeper said, "A little girl about the jumble sale." The term seemed to amuse the old gentleman and he said, "Bring her in and she can tell me what a 'jumble' is." My hermit was having tea and soon I was sitting at the table explaining all about the jumble sale and eating hot scones and homemade jam. Somehow the conversation turned to history and Napoleon was mentioned. Imagine my awe when my hermit told me that as a very small boy he had been taken by his father to see the "Little Corporal" lying in state in St. Helena. I have often thought how few generations it takes to span so many years.

When a real girls' school opened near our house it was decided I should attend, but I was well informed as to how much it would cost and how hard I must work. It was, I think, quite a blow to my parents when my application was refused! The school was only for boarders. Finally, it was agreed that I could start as the only daygirl, on the understanding that I stayed to mid-day dinner and left the premises immediately after school. I enjoyed the thrill of being taught, which reminded me of Byron House and, realizing how backward I was, I know I worked hard. After a year and a half, my parents went to Switzerland and I spent the summer term of 1907 as a boarder. I shall never forget the journey I made from Crowborough to Winchelsea where we had a summer cottage. I was, after all, only thirteen, and I had to make a train journey necessitating two changes at Lewes and Hastings and, in addition to my school trunk and overnight case, I had a tennis racquet, hockey stick, violin, and a bicycle. To add to this list, I had to pick up our cat who had recently had kittens and our dog Jack who had been boarded with the gardener. I still think I did well to arrive some hours later, with everything but the bicycle, which had been left behind in Hastings. I loved Winchelsea and Rye. A number of well-known artists had homes there. Ellen Terry had a cottage in Winchelsea, and Archie Marshall, a well-known novelist of the time, lived at Rye. I spent a lot of time with his daughters and we were joined in any picnics and games by G. K. Chesterton, and I also met H. G. Wells at the Marshalls.

At this time, my younger brother was learning his trade with the Deasy Motor Car Company in Coventry, and during August he and a mechanic were sent to deliver two cars to some people named Orman who had recently moved into a house near the village of Liphook in Hampshire. Arrangements had been made for the expected two mechanics to lodge with the Orman's two chauffeurs, but when my brother arrived Mrs. Orman, I think, felt both he and the other three men might feel slightly embarrassed, and arrangements were altered and Ronald joined the Orman family and was soon playing tennis and swimming and fishing with the Orman's fourteen-year-old daughter, Rotha. One evening, Mrs. Orman happened to mention that she had engaged a governess for Rotha and was hoping to find a girl to share her lessons. My brother said he had a sister of the same age as Rotha with the same outdoor tastes, and I was invited to spend two weeks of my holidays at Forest Mere.

My brother and Rotha drove over in the touring car to collect me, but I never thought as I climbed in that it would be many years before I was to really live at home again. I was, too, rather resentful at being, as I thought, pushed off onto complete strangers when I was so enjoying my freedom at Winchelsea. The style in which the Ormans lived was so different from anything I had experienced that I hated my first few days and blamed my brother for letting me in for two weeks of such misery. My clothes, for one thing, were all wrong, and I was bitterly ashamed of my underclothes made from some fine linen chemises which had belonged to my grandmother, and I envied Rotha her liberty bodices and suspenders instead of the garters which held up my long, thick, black stockings. Rotha wore linen blouses and skirts, no stockings, and sandals. Meals, too, were agony. I had never had to help myself from silver dishes handed over my left shoulder, and as dinner every night consisted of soup, fish, an entrée, and a main dish, sweet, savoury, and dessert, the array of cutlery put me in a panic. But however hard I tried to dislike everything and everybody, it would have been impossible, I think, to bear resentment towards the Ormans. In no way did they appear to notice my extreme gaucheness, if that is the word, or seem to compare me to their own sophisticated daughter who had, after all, played with the children of the then Prince of Wales, travelled all over Europe, and been on a Mediterranean cruise. She had met all the military men who had come to visit her grandfather Field Marshal Sir Lintorn Simmons, Queen Victoria's favourite Field Marshal, who was a friend and advisor to the Empress Eugenie (widow of Napoleon III) and guardian of her son, the Prince Imperial.

By the end of the second week, however, I was feeling much more at home in my surroundings and was able to chat easily with

Kitty, my personal maid, who was also the head housemaid. The indoor staff consisted of eleven: Mrs. Fox, the cook, and her kitchen and scullery maids, two parlourmaids, the senior of whom also valeted Major Orman, three housemaids, and John, the odd-job man who attended to the artesian well and drove the pony cart into Liphook every morning and evening to collect the papers and letters. There was also a boy from the Gordon Boys' Home, a charity in which Sir Lintorn and the Ormans took a deep interest. The lads only stayed about six months, but were well trained in the fundamentals of service in big establishments. They learned how to wait at table, look after a gentleman's clothes, clean silver, announce visitors, and so on, and Mrs. Orman kept in touch with many of the boys after they left.

One day after lunch Mrs. Orman told Rotha to go and get the boats out, and she took me into her sitting room. She asked if I had enjoyed the holiday and when I said I had, she asked if I would like to spend the next year or two doing lessons with Rotha and going away on holidays abroad. She said she had not approached my parents, as she considered I was the one most affected and there-fore the one whose wishes should be considered first. If I decided to return to school, she would not write to my mother but she knew Rotha would be happy to see me whenever visits could be arranged. I had never been consulted in such a way before, but now I was told to think about the idea and if I liked, talk it over with Rotha. She dismissed me by saying she had heard that we had wheedled an old sheet out of Mrs. Pendergast who looked after the household linen and that we intended to hoist a sail on the gig. "If you must fall overboard," she added, "try to avoid the muddy patch at the end of the lake!" Naturally, I told Rotha at once and she said the idea had come originally from her, for we really had got on so well and had such fun together, she would love me to stay on—and so I did. I think I grew up a lot during that visit, for I began to have more confidence in myself. Hitherto I had always been able to talk easily with people such as the milkman, the shopkeepers, and gardeners, but I was shy and tongue-tied with visitors in my own home.

Before our governess arrived, Mrs. Orman, or Aunt Blanche as I was asked to call her, took Rotha and myself to London to buy clothes. We stayed at the Savoy, and it was the first time I had ever been in a hotel of that size and I was amazed at the self-confident way in which Rotha ordered tea in the lounge soon after we arrived. Next morning we shopped, first at Nobles in the Burlington Arcade for blouses, and then at Debenham and Freebody. When I realized that warm underclothes and sweaters were being added to my order, I ventured to protest that I felt my parents could not afford such expenses, but Aunt Blanche explained that she and my mother had agreed that as long as I lived at Forest Mere, she would be responsible for my wardrobe, and so it was!

Apart from our ski outfits and schoolroom clothes—navy skirts and navy or white Viyella blouses —Rotha and I were never dressed the same. Our best evening and dance dresses were Swiss silk, made by Edith in different styles; Rotha's had edelweiss and mine had snowdrops embroidered on the skirt and bodice. Soon after our return our governess, Miss Knox-Coffer, arrived. We were rather in awe of her at first as she was inclined to sing the praises of her late pupil, the titled daughter of an Irish earl. Why we called her the Basilisk, I can't remember. I had, by this time, given up all hope of ever going to a real school, and Rotha and I settled down to a routine of doing as little learning as possible and enjoying ourselves.

One day we all drove to some kennels to choose our dogs. Aunt Blanche had had a St. Bernard called Queenie for many years, but Queenie had died just before they moved. Now she wanted another of the same breed and the friend who kept the kennels thought he had the right one in Duchess. Rotha and her father wanted fox terriers and I was asked if I had any special choice and, if not, would I see if I would like to own a lovely Great Dane who was said to be very much a "one-man dog?" This proved to be true, and from the moment we were introduced to Czar, as I named him, he was my shadow and I was thrilled when his new collar arrived engraved "Nesta Maude, Forest Mere." He had many engaging habits, the most intriguing being that when I knelt at the bedside to say my prayers, Czar would sometimes heave his front paws onto the bed beside me and lay his head down on them. Rotha's rough-haired terrier was called Dapper Dandy but answered to Dandy, and although he was an attractive and obedient dog, he did not give her the same devotion that Czar gave to me.

CHAPTER II:

Girl Scouts
1908–1909

After the Boer War, Lord Baden-Powell, the hero of the Relief of Mafeking, outlined a scheme for training boys to become good citizens by encouraging discipline, unselfishness, and self-reliance. In 1907, he put the scheme into action by running the first Boy Scout camp on Brownsea Island off the coast of Dorset, and the movement was born. At that time he did not envisage a similar organization for girls. He was to say later, "I started the Boy Scouts, but you girls started yourselves." One of these early founders of the Girl Guides was Nesta Maude.

In the autumn of 1908 Rotha and I started to go to Confirmation Classes with the Rev. Bland at Milland Vicarage. There were several other girls of our age, and classes were held on Saturday mornings as we all had to walk across the moors, which would have been impossible after dark. The Confirmation was to be held on November 8 by the Bishop of South Tokyo, an Englishman presumably retired or on leave from his See in Japan. That morning Aunt Blanche gave me an Anglican prayer book, Uncle Charlie the matching hymnbook, and Rotha's gift was a Roman Catholic missal, which she knew I should need when we travelled abroad. I soon learned that no matter what country we were in, on Sundays we always attended the local church service. It might be Anglican or Roman Catholic, or even Lutheran. The Ormans themselves were High Church, or Anglo-Catholic as they were termed in those days, and Forest Mere contained a beautiful little chapel under the big staircase in which prayers were read every morning for any of the staff and visitors who cared to attend, but they were tolerant and understanding of other Christians whose chosen way of worship was different from the service of their personal choice.

My elder brother, who was a journalist, came from London for the day to represent my family, and as a Confirmation gift he gave me a rather grubby copy of a paperback book called *Scouting for Boys*. The gift was made just before I went to my room to change for my Confirmation, and as I propped it up on the dressing table it opened to something called the Scout Law. By the time we got to church I found I could repeat these Laws and it seemed quite in order that the Bishop's address should stress the importance of having certain standards by which to live. My brother's present, which had actually been handed to him to review and which he had read on the train journey, became the open sesame to two girls who might otherwise easily have fallen into the state of being bored and selfish.

As winter grew near, the joys of the lake, swimming, fishing, canoeing, and exploring lost their attraction and we were reduced to tramping over the moors with the dogs. One of our favourite haunts was the little island in the middle of the lake and we used to sit on the branch of the only tree, our heads close together, both reading out of this fascinating book, *Scouting for Boys*. One day we read about building a hut and one of us said, "Why don't we build a hut here on the island?" and that for me was the start of a life-long connection with the Scout and Guide Movements. We invested our pocket money in an axe and scoured the woods for suitable poles for a framework. We had to buy a trowel with which to dig the holes and we ferried boatloads of dry heather for thatching. The first person we allowed to see our "masterpiece" was Rotha's godfather, Major Nason, V.C., a man for whom we both had the greatest admiration. After giving everything a thorough test, he congratulated us on building well and truly and using materials available just for the looking. "Now," he said, "build a proper fireplace and a better landing place for visitors like me." The Major had a game leg and had certainly had difficulty getting from boat to land. We started at once to draw up plans and collect materials for both of these projects, but by the end of the month we were in Switzerland and I was having my first experience of foreign travel and winter sports. Rotha was quite a fair skier and was very good and patient with my efforts, and we were soon able to enjoy the sport, although I think we enjoyed our "luges" or toboggans more than our skis. The highlight came when we had the temerity to enter a race and won it, which to our great astonishment gave us the Championship of Canton de Vaud! I imagine the race must have been for fifteen-year-old entrants, but I remember people clapping for us as we went in to dinner that night. Even better was the thrill of dancing with a young naval cadet, my first heart-throb, and being completely tongue-tied until we found a common subject in signalling and created slight amusement by standing up and doing semaphore to each other. The lad fortunately had a friend who had met Rotha and the four of us made a very happy quartet.

Returning to Forest Mere we made up our minds to get properly enrolled as Scouts, but we were taking in a weekly paper called *The Scout* and several references to enrolments seemed to make it clear that girls could not be Scouts. We felt sure we could pass all the necessary Tenderfoot Tests, but the knots puzzled us a bit, and I remember sitting on the stable wall with bits of string and trying to follow the intricacies of the bowline. Our second chauffeur, who also attended to the electric light engine, was an old sailor and our fumbling efforts were too much for him. "Look," said the voice of authority, "a bowline is for hauling a body up a cliff or letting them down over a ship's side, and not for doing up parcels, and you tied it in rope and in the dark likely and with one hand!" and with that he taught us to whip and splice ropes and I can truly say our knots were well tied. Having satisfied ourselves that we had completed all the requirements for the Tenderfoot Test, we compiled a letter to Scout Headquarters requesting the registration of the Forest Mere Troop of "Scouts," all reference to sex omitted! This masterpiece of composition was signed N. Maude and Assistant R. Orman. To our delight the letter was accepted as we hoped and back came a little certificate of registration, a request for some money, and a catalogue and price list of Scout uniform and equipment. The latter interested us enormously and we spent hours poring over the fascinating pictures of tents, billycans, and water bottles, not to mention tracking irons which left the slot of a deer or mark of a horse's hoof. The catalogue, as much as anything, made us think seriously about getting other girls to join us and to form a proper Troop, something that would certainly need parental approval! I think we were both surprised to find out how much Mrs. Orman already knew about Scouting. She had read our Scout magazine and had heard from the Commandant of the Longmoor Mounted Infantry Camp of the formation of a Troop of Boy Scouts in the neighbourhood, to which many of the boys from the Married Quarters belonged. Not only did both she and the Major give their whole-hearted support to the idea of forming a Troop, but Mrs. Orman agreed to become Scout Mistress. We had noticed in *The Scout* that many Troops were led by women, so there was no need to conceal the fact that she was "Mrs.", and if references were needed I am sure that the Rector, whose daughter was one of our earliest recruits, or any of the local Military would have obliged.

One afternoon Rotha and I visited the principals of two schools which lay about two miles on either side of Forest Mere, one in Liphook and one in the smaller village of Liss that the children from Rake also attended. Both men were quite knowledgeable about Scouting and felt it might appeal to some girls, but they thought we would be wise to stress to the parents the more womanly aspects of the training such as cooking and nursing. Mr. Hillier, whose daughter Evelyn joined on the first day, was delighted at the idea that we hoped to teach the girls to swim and row in the summer, but warned us that the parents might be horrified at the suggestion, and as for sleeping in a tent he laughed and said, "Forget it!" We left notices to be read to the school assembly saying, "Any girls between the ages of eleven and fourteen who are interested in becoming Girl Scouts are invited to come to Forest Mere at one o'clock next Saturday afternoon. Milk and buns will be provided." We wrote and re-wrote our program for Saturday, but fortunately realized in time that what we were planning was just a showing off of activities which we enjoyed doing, and the role of the girls would be to watch and think how clever we were! We scrapped everything and started again.

We had, of course, no idea how many or how few girls would come, but the sight of two little groups of four approaching from each direction filled us with excitement. First, we showed some pictures of sailors doing semaphore, and having divided the girls into pairs we gave each one a card with a few easy letters made by "pin men" with their arms in the correct positions. One girl was told to pick out letters spelling the name of an animal and to send it to her partner who was to acknowledge it by making the noise of the animal. My heart leapt when I heard the first tentative "meow," but soon all eight girls caught on and the air was filled with hoots, barks, moos, and so on. Then some girls made dampers or bannocks, others found big stones and built fireplaces, and others collected wood and learned what and what not to use to start a fire.

Soon a billycan of water was boiling and the bannocks were rising. A message was taken to our Scout Mistress who came attended by Czar who, like the perfect gentleman he always was, allowed himself to be hugged and loved and was unanimously adopted as Troop Mascot. I must confess, we cheated a bit in providing self-rising flour for our bannocks and a little butter to go with them, and also milk and sugar for our tea! Mrs. Orman, in a few words, spoke of the Aims of Scouting, and then she taught us all a simple round in two parts. Our first Scout meeting— or Parade, as we called it—ended with the singing of "God Save the King" and the Lord's Prayer. After milk and buns to sustain them on the walk home, the girls were told to think about scouting and if they liked the idea to come again next week and bring a friend, then we would have two full patrols and could choose our animal names.

The following Saturday we nearly doubled our numbers and had visions of a third patrol. Strangely enough, although Forest Mere existed for four years, one year as a Troop of Girl Scouts and for three as a Company of Girl Guides, it always consisted of just two patrols averaging eight or nine girls each. The idea of a third patrol cropped up from time to time during the four years, but many of our girls left school at fourteen and either went into service or left home to continue their education elsewhere. At that second Parade we did a little First Aid and some knots. The latter we always taught in a practical setting, and while my group put up clotheslines with a clove hitch and joined two cords with a reef knot, Rotha's was demonstrating tying a bundle of logs together with a round turn and two half hitches. We were at this time attending St. John's Ambulance First Aid Classes and thus managed to keep one jump ahead of the girls. The examination came the day after my sixteenth birthday, and although we both passed with no difficulty, I was awarded the Senior Certificate, while Rotha, a month younger, only got the Junior, although she had taken the Senior Course and Examination.

We divided the training between us fairly evenly. I took the First Aid and Signalling and Nature while Rotha had all the Drills and Camp Crafts such as tracking, fires, hut building, and so on. I tried always to make my First Aid accidents look as real as possible and sometimes I would leave it to one girl to stage an emergency that had to be diagnosed and treated by the other patrol. On one occasion a girl managed to stick a little bit of bone to her shin surrounded by a little scarlet grease paint. This was greeted by shrieks of delight and the information that it was a "constipated fracture." I had a reputation for saying, "But suppose you had not got so-and-so?" On one occasion my corporal (or second) was in a wood dealing with a simulated fractured tibia. She had splinted the leg with a branch, her tie, handkerchief, and both stockings and as I came up to criticize she burst out, "For goodness' sake, don't say what would I do if there weren't any trees, 'cos there aren't any umbrellas or newspapers handy, and surely accidents must happen convenient-like sometimes!" Some fifty years after the Forest Mere Scouts ceased to exist, I had a letter from one of the girls who thought I would be interested to know our nicknames of that time. I was, it seems, known as the Lovable Bear and Rotha was the Tiger!

As Longmoor Mounted Infantry Camp lay just across the moor, our Scout Mistress arranged with the Commandant for Sergeant Payne to come over sometimes on a Saturday and teach us Morse signalling and how to march and form fours and so on. We all loved "Sarge," as we called him, and sometimes he would bring a friend who had served abroad and they would tell us stories of active service in India and Africa. One visitor had actually served with the Chief Scout in the Siege of Mafeking, so of course he became a hero himself to our eleven year olds! Rotha and I spent one rather unhappy day as the result of our enthusiasm for signalling. We had made ourselves a heliograph apparatus and were out on the moor in the sunshine flashing our signals. It so happened that a detachment of the Mounted Infantry was exercising on the moor at the same time. One of the young NCOs, whose Morse was probably not as good as ours, misread the flashes as an instruction to take his small command back to camp—which he did! The result was an exchange of letters between Commandant and Scout Mistress, and I suspect some amusement in the canteen and Officers' Mess!

When the weather became warm enough, we offered to teach any girl who wanted to learn how to swim, but we insisted that they must have their parent's consent and also a note from a doctor. Very few of the girls had ever been in water other than the once-a-week tin tub in front of the kitchen fire, and loud were the squeals as they waded into the cold lake. I doubt if they learned much swimming, but they certainly learned their artificial respiration under most realistic conditions. First, a limp (probably giggling!) patient would be taken from the water with a bit of duckweed draped over her face. The old-fashioned Schafer method of resuscitation would be started and another girl would be dispatched to the house. Although Forest Mere was not on the telephone, we had obtained a dummy one and every girl could use it. She had to notify the doctor, police, parents and hospital with Mrs. Orman listening to check that she spoke clearly and gave information to everyone sensibly. One or two other girls would also go to the house and would have to make up a bed with blankets and hot water bottles and be ready to answer questions about food and aftercare. The exercise would end with the improvisation of a stretcher from two coats and Scout poles, or a hurdle, and the transportation of the patient to safety.

We wanted to have our own prayer but, of course, there was no Guide Prayer in those days. We got hold of a lot of bookmarks on which was printed the following prayer, which I think is a very fine prayer for Guides:

I shall pass through this
world but once. Any good
therefore that I can do or
any kindness that I can
show to any human being,
let me do it now. Let me
not defer or neglect it for
I shall not pass this way
again.

We used to repeat this prayer every meeting before we dismissed.

In the spring of 1909, Rotha and I were filled with the desire to camp for a week on the little island in the middle of the big lake. We had followed Major Nason's advice and built a good jetty and a fireplace on which we often cooked our catch of perch, tench, and the occasional trout. At one time we were told the lake was well stocked with trout, but the building of Longmoor Camp and the mounted troops' activities had blocked the little streams that used to run into the lake and gradually the trout were dying out. At first, our request for permission to sleep out was received with a flat "No," but after the Major had inspected "One Tree Island," as we called our domain, leave was given with two conditions: first, that we take enough tinned food to ensure that we could have a good hot meal once a day; and second, that we hoist a flag morning and evening. The flag was to be red if all was well, yellow if we were coming back, and black if we wanted help, in which case, I imagine, one of the men would come dashing out in a canoe. Privately and to ourselves, we made other conditions, the first being not to open a single tin but to live off the land, and the second to take with us only the bare necessities, such as we imagined the pioneers and explorers in Canada and Africa would have taken. Our list consisted of such things as flour, tea, bacon, and salt. We had made friends with the gamekeeper on a neighbouring estate and he had not only shown us how to snare a rabbit, but had frequently taken us out in the woods in the evening to watch a vixen and her cubs, and I remember lying on my stomach peering over a bank for what seemed like hours but being rewarded by Brock the Badger stealing out for his evening hunt. This man was only one of several experts we asked to come and talk to our Scouts, and he taught us such things as the difference between edible and inedible mushrooms and fungi and the danger of eating poisonous berries like deadly nightshade.

We always tried to keep in mind that we were country-dwellers and the emergencies we were most likely to meet with would be connected with animals or possibly farm implements. Many a man has had to lie up as the result of having his foot stepped on by a large carthorse, and a bite from any animal needs immediate attention, as does even the simplest scratch from a farm cat if infection is to be avoided. One of our most useful sources of information of this sort was the cowman at the nearby Home Farm, and it was from him that the suggestion came that we should learn to milk a cow. This we had done some months before we even thought of camping, but the Bailiff said if we were to get up by 6:00 a.m. we might have the milk from one cow—provided we milked and fed her ourselves. This offer started us on a hunt for a shallow pan in which we could cool our milk and a wide-mouthed jar in which to churn butter. Oh yes, we made it, not perhaps up to the Dairy Show standard, but it spread and made our daily bannocks more palatable.

The Camp was to last from after church on Sunday to the following Saturday afternoon. By five o'clock we had moved into our temporary home and had caught and cleaned the fish, which with wild raspberries was to be our supper. I doubt if either of us slept very well that first night, but we were up in time to keep our appointment with Bessie, the cow. We planned to take it in turns to be milker and

I had drawn the first morning while Rotha got breakfast, which on this first morning was to be bacon and mushrooms. The snares we had set the day before produced nothing and we lunched off bannocks and hard-boiled moorhens' eggs, with fish again for supper. Next morning, I had the thrill of finding a nice, plump bunny in our snare, and our meat ration was assured. We were very conscious of the necessity of eating vegetables and fresh fruit as a preventive measure against scurvy and we spent hours picking young nettles. The first time we were horrified to see how they boiled down, leaving just a small helping each from the huge panful we had picked. Provided one wears gloves and is careful to avoid the dark, older leaves, which are bitter, they make an excellent substitute for spinach. The rabbit gave us two good meals each and with bacon and mushrooms we stretched it to three.

When we suggested the camp, several people said we would be back in two days. "You'll be bored to tears with nothing to do," they said, but we never seemed to be idle. We swam, of course, once or twice a day and started to make a detailed chart of the lakeshore showing all the little bays and creeks where the streams used to trickle in from the moor. Actually, there were two lakes joined by a channel and the land between them was heavily wooded and at one point only a few yards from the mainland. It was while we were exploring round the little lake that we found a submerged kayak canoe. The salvaging of this treasure took us nearly a whole day. We got it out of the water and mud after a struggle and upended it on two stumps to drain. Some weeks later we succeeded in making this boat more or less seaworthy with the aid of wool and tar and canvas patches, but it was never very reliable. A second kayak we found in some bushes later on was in much better shape and gave us a lot of fun and made a change from the Indian canoes, which we both possessed. So the days passed and apart from our trips to the mainland for food such as moorhens' eggs, mushrooms, bilberries, raspberries, and of course, the milk, we never left the lake. The red flag was religiously hoisted twice a day, every tin of food was returned unopened, and everyone laughed when we confessed that the only thing we had forgotten to take was a tin opener!

CHAPTER III:

The Crystal Palace Rally
1909–1910

The London Times newspaper for Monday, September 6, 1909, contained the following item:

Boy Scouts' Rally

The first annual rally of boy scouts took place at the Crystal Palace on Saturday, and the building and grounds on the occasion very much resembled a large camping arena. There were no fewer than 11,000 scouts present from all parts of Great Britain, and amongst them was a troop of girl scouts, who excited considerable curiosity.

. . . General Baden-Powell took his stand on the platform below the great organ during the march past, which occupied three-quarters of an hour. The girl scouts were loudly cheered as they passed.

The presence of girls forced Lord Baden-Powell to set up an organization for them and he asked his sister, Miss Agnes Baden-Powell, to take charge of it.

During the summer of 1909 we toured Brittany by car and had a wonderful time. Aunt Blanche always realized that sitting in a car all day, however lovely the scenery, was no fun for a restless energetic couple of teenagers, and she never tried to restrain our activities. As long as we had some money, a map, and a rough route worked out, we were free to explore the Breton villages and make friends with the fishermen in their boats and the farmers and their wives in the markets. When we returned home, the Scouting world was full of news of the coming Rally to be held at the Crystal Palace in September. Some years later the Chief told me that when the idea was first suggested, many guesses were made on the number of boys who might be expected. These varied from five hundred to two thousand, but no one in the Scout hierarchy expected anything like the eleven thousand lads who came from every corner of the United Kingdom to meet their Chief. No mention was made in *The Scout* of girls attending, but our Scout Mistress agreed to send by car any Forest Mere girls who wished to go to the Crystal Palace. Rotha and I were rather surprised that there were no takers, but it was, of course, the parents' decision, and if we had been more experienced we would have visited the mothers personally and explained what a Rally was all about! In spite of our disappointment, Rotha and I set off full of excitement at the prospect of seeing the Chief Scout in person, but with no idea that we would be taking part in what to the Girl Guide Movement proved to be an historic event.

It was not a nice day; cold, windy, and drizzly, the sort of day in fact that came to be known in Scout circles as the "Chief's weather." Baden-Powell used to say he arranged it that way in order to give the Scouts a chance to keep their Law and sing and whistle at all times. Certainly no amount of rain could have dampened the spirits of the thousands of lads who swung into the Palace grounds, heads up and shoulders squared! For many of them it was their first impression of the size of the organization to which they belonged. There had been smaller Rallies, of course, county ones of a few hundred boys perhaps, but this was the first time London East Enders had seen Scottish Scouts and one kilted Troop I remember came in for much admiration. Rotha and I marched confidently up to the entrance, only to be told quite firmly by a marshal that we could not join the Rally. We protested that we were Scouts, but the marshal only smiled and said we could go and sit in the stands and watch everything, but we could not take part. We did not argue, but when the next Troop of boys approached and marched through the gate, whether they knew it or not they had two camp followers on the gate marshal's blind side! Once inside no power on earth would have got us out of the Rally, but we were at a loss as to where we should stand. There were other girls in uniform; a few seemed unattached as we were, but there were a few sizable detachments that were calling themselves by names other than Scouts, such as "Girls Emergency Corps." These organized parties took part in the March Past, but Rotha and I joined about fifteen other girls and watched, wishing we had the right to march with the boys. Who actually approached the Chief with the request that he should come and inspect us, I have no idea, but soon it was obvious that the moment we hoped for was going to happen and we were going to meet our Chief in person! As the great man came towards our little group we wondered if he would speak to us, but of course his opening words, so often quoted, "Who are you?" gave us the reply we were all longing to give: "We're the Girl Scouts." That, of course, put the ball squarely in the Chief's court and he returned it. "You can't be; there aren't any Girl Scouts." Back came the answer, "Oh yes there are, 'cos we're them!"

To quote an article by Alix Liddell in the *Diamond Jubilee Souvenir* book, "There comes a time when a good soldier knows he is beaten and Baden-Powell was a good soldier," and two months later a pamphlet was published giving an outline of training for girls. By

February 1910, it seemed as though very soon the new Girl Guides Organization would be as firmly established as its counterpart, the Boy Scouts, especially as it started with a foundation of six thousand members who, many of them reluctantly, agreed to transfer their allegiance and to drop their self-given name of Girl Scouts becoming instead Girl Guides. The title, which is the name of a famous Indian regiment, was chosen by the Chief Scout who gave as his reason for the choice not only the regiment's outstanding military record, but also its well-known ability to cope with any emergency and the loyalty and honesty of every soldier in its ranks. These, said the Chief, were the qualities he hoped to see developed in both Scouts and Guides.

We accepted the new name, but not the fact that the Chief was no longer *our* Chief, for he had handed over the leadership of the infant guide movement to his sister, Miss Agnes Baden-Powell, and the change was not popular. Moreover, she was a "President" which put her in the category of an elderly lady heading the committee which ran the local YWCA or the Flower Show, which as events proved is rather what she was. She was the only girl in a family of boys and had been educated privately, and although she was very artistic and a fine musician, she had never mixed with other girls and knew nothing of the growing up problems of teenagers—or "flappers" as they called us in the early 1900s. The committee members Miss Agnes gathered around her were well-known names but, again, elderly ladies whose own daughters, after a strict Victorian upbringing, had long since married and flown the coop! Rotha and I wished our Scout Mistress had been on that committee. But almost the next best thing happened, for Miss Agnes invited Rotha and me to tea at her house in Prince's Gate where she and her mother lived. I remember the beautifully composed and rather stilted letter now, and it certainly was not one to make two fifteen year olds feel at ease. We were left at the door and told the car would call for us in one and a half hours. The first shock was to find birds flying around the entrance hall and the staircase as we were shown up to the drawing room to be greeted by Miss Baden-Powell and introduced to several other ladies. They all asked us a lot of questions about the Troop and had we taught our girls to sew (the last thing either one of us was qualified to teach!). Did the girls know about health rules and brushing their teeth and did we go for nature walks and picnics? We tried to get the conversation onto the joys of tracking and lighting fires and camping, but somehow it was always played back with "We must remember we are a girls movement and not copy boys!" For some reason, "boys" always seemed to be spoken as if it was not a very nice word. Rotha said on the way home her lady made them sound a bit slimy, like slugs. When the door opened and the Chief himself walked in and shook hands with the ladies and returned our salutes, we told him we had been at the Crystal Palace and he said he was glad we were Guides and then he excused himself and made a little bow to the company and left.

When we heard that a book similar to *Scouting for Boys* was being written for girls, we were thrilled. In the meantime, two pamphlets were published giving details of correct uniform, badge tests, and so on. "Pamphlet B" opens with the following words: "Girls, imagine a battle has taken place in your village. Are you going to wring your hands and cry, or are you going to be brave and go out and help your fathers and brothers who are falling for you?" We were then shown the importance of tracking and first aid so as to search out and bring in the wounded. Signalling was to be used to call up the doctor, and cooking must be learned in order to make stews or poultices for the injured! The Chief Scout had always been so careful to avoid any suggestion of militarism in Scouts' training that many of the original Girl Scouts were frankly horrified. The wording too was rather over the head of the average eleven year old. Rotha and I had to explain that to "wring one's hands" had nothing to do with the mangle they all no doubt had to turn on washing days! Actually, owing to Miss Baden-Powell's illness, *How Girls Can Help to Build the Empire*, which was the rather grandiose title of the new publication, was delayed until May 1912. This was probably just as well, as the effect of "Pamphlet B" had had time to be forgotten, although the war theme reappeared with all its gruesome and amusing details. I have often read the story of the battle to present day Guides and they have laughed as we did at the thought of two small Guides bringing in a six-foot Guardsman, and we so hoped the doctor could read Morse, and we liked poultices being included in the Cook's Badge. I fear *How Girls Can Help to Build the Empire* was never taken very seriously as a training manual, and most ex-Scouts and early Guide Mistresses relied on *Scouting for Boys* for training and campfire yarns.

With the thrill of the Crystal Palace Rally behind us, Rotha and I gave ourselves to training the two patrols of the Forest Mere Company. Looking back over the years and reviewing what I have seen of the other groups, it would have been hard to find a smarter more efficient body of girls, none of whom was over fourteen! Of course, that is easy to say, for we had no competition and it is really pure conceit on my part! Seriously though, I often feel that Guiding over the years has tended to drift away from the basic fundamentals laid down by the Chief. The hamper for the needy family—for which parents buy tins of food or flowers—given by the Company has too often taken the place of the personal kind action we thought so important. One of the disappointing things about becoming Guides was the loss of the big Scout scarves, which were replaced by pale blue ties. They were half the size of our old red ones and useless for making a stretcher. We used to knot the ends together until a good turn had been performed and then untied them and let them flap.

As the winter of 1910 approached, Parade was changed from 2:00 p.m. to 10:00 a.m. and we all worked hard to convert an old loft into a workable club house for wet days, for bad weather never seemed to deter the girls from turning up on Saturdays. We also started work on our Colours. After much discussion, we decided on a square, rather than rectangular, flag. It was divided diagonally, one half scarlet for the Pimpernels and the other Sunflower yellow. In the centre was a white lozenge with a green trefoil. The flag was mounted on a white staff topped by a gold trefoil cut out of tin. When finished, the flag looked very bare and obviously needed a finish, and we were delighted to be offered a job by a farmer who agreed to pay us to clear out his barn. It was dirty work, but sixteen pairs of hands made for a good job and the result was enough gold fringe to make our Colours look very handsome. Next came the question of selecting a Colour Bearer. We gave each girl a paper and agreed that we would all write the name of the Guide we thought best lived up to the Guide Laws and qualities expected of a Girl Guide. The slips, unsigned, were dropped into a sealed box through a slit and handed to our Guide Mistress who announced later that Winnie Woods of my Sunflowers was an almost unanimous choice.

Here, I must leap forward seventy years to complete the story. I was driving across Canada with my elder daughter and we were being entertained in Regina by the Provincial Commissioner and some of the Executive Committee. I had been talking of those early days and had passed round the enrolment card issued to me in 1910 with the Company name of Forest Mere, Liphook. Suddenly, one of the Brownie Guiders let out a cry of "My mother lives in Liphook, and my Aunt belonged to that Company!" So I learned that our one-time Colour Bearer had married a Canadian soldier after the First War and had died not so many years ago. Rotha's Pimpernel Corporal, Christine Ayling, became nursemaid to my nephew, now the Rt. Hon. Angus Maude, M.P., retired Paymaster

General. Some years ago when Angus was speaking somewhere, he was told by someone after the meeting that they had overheard a lady in the row behind telling a friend that she had been nurse to the Member. Angus always regretted he had not followed the matter up as he had very fond memories of Christine. The news of my Sunflower Corporal, Maggie Windibank, I obtained sometime in the late 50s when I met a Guider in British Columbia married to a Royal Canadian Mounted Police officer. She had been a Barnardo Girl and remembered the name of Miss Windibank as a Home Mother at the Girls Village Home.

Rotha and I had known since Christmas that we were to spend the summer in Oberammergau, the little Bavarian village where the Passion Play is performed every ten years by the villagers in fulfilment of the vow made 350 years ago by their forebears. In 1632 that most dreaded of all infectious illnesses, the Black Death, was sweeping across Europe and more than seventy people in the village had already died. The villagers swore they would write and perform a play depicting the Passion of Christ every ten years if God would halt the advance of the plague. No more people died, several who were already ill recovered, and the vow has been faithfully kept every decade since. I had never heard of the Passion Play. My parents being very Low Church, my only contact with religion was a long and somewhat dreary service of one and a half hours on Sunday mornings. Sometimes my mother would whisper, "Father and I are staying to Second Service. Go straight home." It never occurred to me to ask what "Second Service" was; I just accepted it as something grown ups did and when my brothers, who were all confirmed at school, also stayed to "Second Service" it was obviously something girls had no part in. Until I went to Forest Mere, I had not heard of Confirmation and it was Rotha who explained to me one day when we were fishing all about High Church or Anglo-Catholics and their use of ritual and Low or Evangelical Services. I think Aunt Blanche was one of the most broad-minded women on the subject of religion. Very High Church herself, if on our travels we were spending a Sunday in a place where the only place of worship was perhaps Lutheran or a tiny Church of England village church, we always attended service. I noticed very early that before starting a meal, Aunt Blanche would make a tiny movement on her rather ample bosom! Rotha explained this to me, as I had never seen people crossing themselves. When we were alone, the Major said Grace but at parties and restaurants this quite unobtrusive movement, as Rotha put it, "shows God we haven't forgotten our manners!"

When we heard that the plan was to drive from Liphook to Bavaria in South Germany we were thrilled. Although we were both under seventeen, we had been driving for over a year. The private driveway from the road was over a mile long and there were plenty of tracks on the moor. I think we both hoped there might come a time when Judd, our excellent chauffeur, would be unable to drive but we never had an opportunity to show our skill at the wheel and it says much for the workmanship of those days that our trip was accomplished without a single mechanical breakdown. What fun we had planning the route and how little of it I remember now! We headed north from Ostend to see something of the bulb fields in Holland, then south through the vineyards of France, stopping in Rheims to visit the champagne cellars. Although Aunt Blanche knew Europe very well, all her travels had been by train or horse-drawn vehicles, and she longed to see how the people lived in the rural areas. Our journey was made before the days of autobahns and traffic lights, and we travelled leisurely through the quiet and less frequented roads. At least once a day Rotha and I would be put down with a map and a route to follow which would bring us to a given rendezvous where we would be picked up by the car. Another walk in the evening gave us the exercise we needed and prevented us from being bored. We frequently slept in lovely village inns, which in those days were delighted to welcome the wealthy English. Both Major and Mrs. Orman had such pleasant manners and the happy knack of expecting the best service and therefore getting it and being willing to pay for it. Languages were no trouble. Judd had a working knowledge of Dutch from service in the South African War. Aunt Blanche was fluent in Italian and French, but I think she underplayed her German in order to make Rotha and me work harder at it! She did, however, insist that we learned all the technical terms for such things as "a puncture," "a jack," "I need a tow truck," and "Where is the garage?"

Our last night on the journey was spent in Munich and the next day we drove up to Oberammergau. It seemed to me the entire village had turned out to greet us. The Ormans had stayed with the Anton Langs on several occasions and were obviously welcome visitors. Anton was the Christus for the second time (a third time in 1922, Ed.) and, according to his granddaughter (who appeared on a televised interview in the 1970s), he is thought to be the finest actor to have played the part. The children gazed open-mouthed at the big motor car and, after the luggage had been unloaded, the Major filled the car with excited youngsters and sent them off in relays with Judd for their first motor car ride. Rotha and I spent the first week getting to know the village and making friends with our own age group. We spent hours watching and talking to men like St. Peter, the best carver, and St. Matthias who was the baker. It seems strange that we knew nearly all the older men only by their play names and I have a photograph signed "To my friend Nesta from St. John."

**Anton Lang, with long hair and beard grown
for his part as the Christus, 1910**

Anton Lang's carving of Christ, 4 1/2"

In 1910, Oberammergau was not the tourist attraction it has since become, but with the advent of motorcars it was obvious that changes were on the way. I have never been back nor would I wish to. I can remember the simple little village with no hotels, and no big shops with plate glass windows. Every home took its quota of visitors and all our friends had their jobs helping at home, and I like to remember that we, too, were accepted and our services used in the same way as the local teenagers! I often swept out the shavings from St. Peter's carvings while Rotha went on errands for Frau Lang. One job we always enjoyed was gathering flowers for the church. There were gentians, kingcups, lupins, columbines, and many blooms I never knew the names of.

One day our party was picnicking halfway up the Kofel and the young members were tobogganing on boards down the short, dry, grassy slope. I was taking a breather and sitting next to Anton when he told me to bring him a little branch from a silver birch tree nearby. Taking out his knife he began to carve the shape of a head. A few days later when Anton gave it to me it was the most exquisite head of Christ, the features very fine and the points of the thorns as sharp as needles. Seventy years of travelling have done little to spoil the expression of the drooping head.

When Mrs. Orman's father, the Field Marshal, retired from the Army, he held several important diplomatic posts, including those of Ambassador Extraordinary and Envoy Plenipotentiary to the Vatican, and Governor of Malta. During those years his daughter met many of the minor royalties and nobility of the then reigning houses of Europe. By 1910, with the advent of motorcars, access to Oberammergau became far easier and Mrs. Orman was of great assistance to Frau Lang with her ability to speak to visitors not only in their own language, but also on their own level. Rotha and I were always expected to greet the more important guests whom we classified as "Shakers or Bobbers" according to whether they warranted a handshake or a curtsey. Would that I could look back to a diary which I never kept, for the only clear memories I have are of a lovely Princess Marie (a Bobber) and an elderly Count Bismarck (a Shaker)!

The man most highly respected and, to a certain extent, feared in the village was the schoolmaster or Herr Direktor, and when one day Rotha and I were stopped in the road by this august being we wondered what we could have done to offend him. When, however, he asked if we would like to do a "small work" for the Play, we were quick to reply, "Ja Bitte, Herr Direktor." The "small work" was to collect the donkey from its paddock and ensure that it was properly saddled and waiting for Anton (the Christus) to ride on in the Palm Sunday entry. Mrs. Orman gave her permission on the condition we awakened ourselves and got dressed in time to attend early Mass, which was obligatory for all those taking part in the Play that day. This attendance at Mass I think was a tradition which seemed to have grown up like so many others, such as making a child miss an appearance in a tableau or crowd scene as punishment for some little naughtiness. Anything in the way of makeup or false hair was forbidden and the men started to grow their hair and beards months before the parts were allotted. Rotha and I often stood at the end of the village to see Zacharias (not his real name) start to run so that he would arrive on stage really panting and out of breath.

After we returned home, two of our Oberammergau friends came to join the staff at Forest Mere. Francesca, who I think played Mary Magdalene, became the under parlourmaid, and Ella, who was the leading contralto in the Chorus, was one of our housemaids. They came to improve their English, but as three of the staff were Irish, Rotha and I had to be sure the girls did not learn their English with a brogue! How we all enjoyed Ella's lovely voice at Sunday evening

"Hymns." After an early cold supper the entire staff, indoor, outdoor, wives, and children, would come into the big hall and sing hymns, which could be chosen by anyone. Aunt Blanche was an accomplished pianist. Rotha and I played first and second violins and the Major conducted and really did wonders with his amateur choir.

CHAPTER IV:

Girl Guides
1910–1912

For the two years following the Crystal Palace Rally Nesta and Rotha ran their own Guide Company at Forest Mere and whenever they could they went camping. In 1911, Nesta became the first Guide in England to win the coveted Silver Fish award. Rose Kerr, in her book The Story of the Girl Guides, wrote: "It was a token of efficiency and ability in a girl who could make her way upstream against a current."

In October 1912, Lord Baden-Powell married Olave St. Clair Soames, thirty years his junior. Nesta and Lady Baden-Powell met briefly that summer but not again until 1916. From then on they met from time to time at Guide events in England and later in Canada, and corresponded until a year or two before Lady Baden-Powell's death.

The only excitement during the winter of 1910 occurred when Forest Mere Guides gave their first entertainment in the Village Hall. The first half consisted of music: a piano solo by Aunt Blanche, a song by Ella, a violin duet, and a professional conjurer whose expenses were paid by Uncle Charlie as his contribution. For the second half of the evening Rotha and I produced a sort of skit. Roller-skating had just become popular and our first scene showed three girls complaining of having nothing to do and being shown how to skate. This resulted in a fall and the timely entry of three Guides who rendered the necessary First Aid. The scenes that followed showed other aspects of Guide training including kindness to animals in which Czar played the star role. The show ended with a tableau of Britannia. The outcome of this effort was that the Company became more widely known and we were asked to take our act to places where Guides were just starting. We made one trip to Alresford, which necessitated two nights out. We slept in a school on straw-filled palliasses and cooked our own meals, good training for our next adventure.

During the spring we stayed in England, mostly in the Lake District. After a week or two in Grasmere we were to move on to the King's Head at Thirlmere. Rotha and I planned to climb up a mountain called The Lion and The Lamb and from its summit we expected to find a track leading down to Thirlmere. Unfortunately, we ran into a heavy mist and when this cleared and we saw a few houses ahead we realized we had followed the wrong trail. The first person we met was a clergyman whom I was to know well some years later when I became his daughter-in-law! John Ashworth had been Vicar of Borrowdale for some years and was much loved by his scattered parishioners. He took us back to the Vicarage where my future mother-in-law and "Granny" to my children fed us while "Gimpa," as his grandchildren were to call him, harnessed old Sandy, his horse, and prepared to drive us part way to Keswick, leaving us only a few miles to cover, and, as a matter of fact, we were offered a lift all the way to Thirlmere.

Reference to my old enrolment card seems to show that the years 1910 and 1911 were indeed busy ones for the Patrol Leaders of the Forest Mere Company. In spite of the fact that for many weeks in the summer of 1910 we were abroad in Oberammergau, I seem to have earned about sixteen badges, and on May 11, 1911, I qualified for the first Silver Fish to be awarded to a Girl Guide, a little whiting with its tail in its mouth. How nearly I missed gaining that much coveted award is shown by the entry on the enrolment card which shows the Matron's badge (which included the holding of the needle-woman's badge) as having been gained on the same day as the Silver Fish. My hand-sewn blouse had failed to pass owing to the fact that I had put the inset sleeves in back to front. I knew that the actual Fish was in the house and arrangements had been made for a General from the nearby military camp to come over to inspect the company and present various badges. Unless my blouse could be passed I should receive only All-round Cords. Discipline in our house was strict and no extension of bedtime could be allowed, but by 6:00 a.m. I was feverishly stitching away and by 8:00 a.m. Tommy, the white pony, and I were on our way to the village dressmaker with a rather crumpled blouse which was finally accepted. It must not be thought that badges were easier to obtain in those days. In fact, I think in some ways tests were harder, although the standard to be reached depended largely on the ideas of the Guide Mistress. It was not enough to know how to do things; they must actually be done in the presence of the tester. The Laundress badge, which I failed twice, consisted of doing the wash for a family of three and included men's stiff collars, men's shirts, and ladies' starched frilly petticoats. The wash we did in the morning, and having dampened and folded the garments we went back either in the evening or the next day to do the ironing, all under the eagle eye of the tester.

L-R: Rotha Orman, Mrs. Orman, Nesta Maude, 1911

Rotha, Nesta and Czar, 1911

It had always been our ambition to take our Guides camping and this was to be the year, but we were quite unable to get the parents to agree to their daughters sleeping under anything but a "good solid roof"! We were terribly disappointed, but Aunt Blanche solved the question by driving down to Worthing with the second chauffeur who was a general handyman and her own maid, Edith. They inspected two or three schools to be let for the summer and finally settled on one, after Smedley had reported that the stove and plumbing was in good order and Edith found the beds and linen clean. There was a small paddock in which we could pitch a tent and most of the girls had a night or two under canvas. We travelled down to Worthing by train, which in itself was an adventure. Several of the girls had never been in a train and very few had seen the sea. We went down on a Saturday and what a busy day we spent learning our new address, writing postcards home, allotting the duties of Cook and Orderly Patrols, and then washing and ironing our ties, steaming and pressing the brims of our blue felt hats, polishing shoes and belts and whitening whistle lanyards.

That afternoon Rotha and I went to call on the Vicar of the church we would be attending the next day. To our joy we found he was the chaplain to the local Territorials and fully conversant with parade services and Colour Ceremonial. He knew all about Scouting and was looking forward to the start of Girl Guides. As far as he knew there were no companies in Worthing but he hoped our visit would give the movement a push in the right direction. After we had arranged one or two slight alterations to the service, we left and hurried back to tell our Sunflowers and Pimpernels that they must expect to be stopped and questioned about Guides and a lot would depend on their behaviour. The next morning we fell in outside our school and marched to church headed by the colour party. Rotha as usual was in command, and Mrs. Orman went by car and was waiting for us at the church. It was a lovely service and we were very proud of our Colour Bearer who dropped on one knee and handed over the flag to the Vicar who treated it with the same respect he would have given to the regimental flag of the Guards. The sermon was short and based on the story of the Good Samaritan and the Vicar made us all laugh by saying we must not expect to find injured Levites everywhere but look for the kindly action that lay close at hand. We left the church before the congregation and were ready to move off when the people began to press round and started to talk to the girls. Mrs. Orman quickly called "Company Attention – Dismiss" and the girls broke ranks and were free to answer the many queries put to them about Guiding. The rest of the "house camp" passed all too quickly. We hiked on the Downs, went out in boats, swam (the swimming pool was more popular than the sea!), learned to roller skate, and paid several visits to the Pierrot show on the beach.

Rotha and I were both now eighteen and we should soon say goodbye to Miss Knox-Cotter, our governess, of whom we were both very fond, although I am sure we disappointed her in our preference for the out-of-doors to the schoolroom! In September we started to take dancing lessons at a house occupied by some people called Turner-Featherstonehaugh, where Lady Hamilton is said to have met Nelson and to have danced on the dining table. The house is now open to the public, but when I visited it in the sixties with my brother the underground ballroom where we danced was not included in the tour. That year I also paid my last visit to the Empress Eugénie. The first time I had been taken to tea with the old lady she had difficulty with my name, which she pronounced as "Nestaire." Aunt Blanche said probably my second name, being French, would be easier and the Empress at once recognized Gervaise and called me "La Petite Huguenot," and so I learned I had French blood in my veins! In those days there was a very firm distinction between a "dance" and a "ball." Rotha and I were old enough to go to dances in private houses and those held at the Royal Military College at

Sandhurst and here I danced more than once with Prince Maurice of Battenberg. The Ormans gave several dances when the big hall was cleared and a band from London played in the balcony. Altogether my last year at Forest Mere was a "fun year" and I think completed the "growing up" process. The Ormans lease would be up at the end of the year and they would be moving to a smaller house at Bournemouth, so just before Christmas 1912, I went back to Crowborough which would now be home until the First World War disrupted so many people's lives.

Rotha and I had two more camps in the summer of 1912 before I left. We had always wanted to camp in the Lake District but backpacking had not been invented in those days and we could think of no way of carting even the minimum of camping gear over the fells. Then Tommy Easton, landlord of the King's Head at Thirlmere, told us of a real gypsy Romany caravan which could be rented by the week and came complete with Briton, a large brown carthorse, warranted quiet and strong. Our plan was to make up a party of six and when we wanted to move, four people would hike while the other two took charge of Briton and the van and moved on to the next camp site by road, meeting up with the walkers at the given spot. We soon made up our party consisting of Margaret Harris, Guide Captain of Richmond, and her friend Jo Blakely, and Mabel Douglas Johnstone, a trained nurse at Banstead Orthopaedic Hospital for Children, which was the first hospital in England to have its own Guide Company. The sixth place was filled by Myra Day, an older Captain from Chester-le-Street in Durham, a coal-mining town. We all knew and loved "Daisy." For many years she had been governess to the big family of the owner of the local collieries, a splendid employer whose relations with his miners were very different from the stories one heard of conditions in other pits.

Caravan Holiday in the Lake District, 1912

Our first day was spent on the road from Keswick to Borrowdale. Rotha and Jo went ahead and found a pleasant camping spot, which we reached about 4:00 p.m. We all had our own jobs and the first night it fell to me to attend to Briton who had to be unharnessed, rubbed down, fed, and watered and turned out to grass by arrangement with Jimmy Plaskett, the farmer on whose land we camped. Margaret, or the Kid as we called her, had brought her ridge tent, which would sleep three. Rotha and Mabel built a fireplace and prepared our supper while Daisy made up the bunk beds in the caravan and got out the plates. After supper we sat round the fire and talked but it had been a long day and we were all ready for early bed.

Next morning we planned to scramble about on Chapel Fell and the lower slopes of Glaramara and get our "walking legs" and we set off about 10:15. As we reached the road through Rosthwaite the coach, which ran daily from Keswick to Buttermere over Honister, passed us. The driver of the four-in-hand waved his whip in greeting and Rotha and I called back to him, "White Hat, Tom." This puzzled everyone, but if you lived in Borrowdale you knew that if Tom wore his white hat it would be a fine day. The coach was just out of sight round a corner when we heard shouts and cries of alarm. Right on the bend was a hay waggon and something on the cart had torn the back seat off the coach precipitating the five passengers onto the road. There we were: five injured patients—six Girl Guides all in full uniform, of course, and one fully trained nurse, but all with St. John Ambulance certificates and with a few bandages! As the accident had happened at the gates of the Vicarage the Vicar, who recognized Rotha and me, and his wife and a good-looking boy ran out to help. The Vicar suggested everyone come into the shade of the Vicarage garden and his wife hastened away to set out chairs and get lemonade and tea ready. The good-looking boy hovered around anxious to help but not quite knowing what to do. Finally he attached himself to my patient and helped her to a chair in the shade of the big trees. The lady had been flung out and in falling had struck her head on the stone wall which bordered the road. She had a bad cut just above the hairline and nasty scrapes and abrasions. The boy fetched me sharp scissors and I cut away the hair and then asked for a bowl of warm water. When it arrived I thought the lad had really been a bit too generous with the carbolic and that it might sting unpleasantly and I asked for a little "pure water." How often in years to come did I hear my husband say, "Get pure water. Your mother doesn't like any other sort!" Yes, eight years later in 1920 I married the good-looking son of the Vicar!

Word was sent for a relief coach and motor transport for the injured to Keswick Hospital. My lady at first suggested she might finish the tour but I advised her to return to her hotel after seeing the doctor (who I felt sure would put in a few stitches) and then lie down in a darkened room. She smiled and said, "That's good advice and if you are ever in Edinburgh I hope you will come and see me," and she handed me a card, "Dr. Mary Gordon, M.D.," one of the best known of the earliest women doctors! We spent three nights in Borrowdale and each evening we strolled up to the Vicarage and listened to Lakeland stories and sang songs ancient and modern round the piano. The Vicar was a remarkable man; a brilliant classical scholar, he read Greek as easily as English. Music on paper meant nothing to him, he could not read a note, but he had only to hear a tune once and he could sit down and play it perfectly. Long before radios were in every house he made himself a crystal and "cats whisker" set and would tune in to the Savoy Orpheum Dance Band and the next night play the same tunes for two hours in the Village Hall for his parishioners. After the accident our party of six seemed to have become seven and even after we moved to other spots the "good-looking young man" seemed to turn up on his bicycle, usually as the bearer of a spice cake or home baked loaf or fruit from the garden. Under his guidance we went over the Honister Slate Quarries and we climbed Scafell and Glaramara, Great Gable and the Langdale Pikes.

When we got home Rotha and I were very pleased to get an invitation to help at a camp of forty girls at Lulworth Cove. The girls, all Guides, were members of an orphanage in Parkstone and one of the people who took an interest in the girls was Miss Olave Soames who had just become engaged to our Chief Scout. This was one of the best-organized camps I have ever been to. Of course, it had one advantage in that the girls had all been subject to a certain amount of discipline, but the Guide leaders were not members of the staff. The cooking was supervised by a New Zealander on two old stoves under a sheet of corrugated iron. Every morning he went off with two or three girls from the Cook patrol in a pony cart to the nearest shops. Here the girls bought everything needed for the next day's menus, paid the bills, and checked the receipts. The commandant explained that it would have been cheaper to buy in large quantities but the girls learned to be selective and balance costs and so on and were so proud after a successful shop. All the shopkeepers were most co-operative and even the smallest girls would have to buy ribbons or crochet cotton, for every child made her own lace collar for the navy blue uniform dress she wore. One day we were told that some of the friends who visited the orphanage were coming to supper the next day. Rotha and I were asked if there was any sort of show the girls could do which would allow most of them to take part. We thought of Morris Dances but we could not teach more than a dozen girls at the most. In the end we decided on fancy marching to the music of mouth organs. Rotha collected about forty girls and lined them up according to size and explained what they would have to do. Meanwhile I bicycled to Wool and bought rolls of tissue paper of every possible colour. A flashlight was part of every girl's camp equipment and we covered every one with coloured paper and secured it with an elastic band. Then we sorted the girls into colours and began to march. Of course, we had no idea how the lights would show when it got dark, but the effect was really quite good and when the Grand Finale showed the whole group all waving their twinkling lights and switching them off at the same moment the girls were well applauded. They crowded round Rotha and me with their comments, "Edie's arm got tired so I held two lights," "Did anyone see Bobby trip over a stone?," "A yellow light got into us Blue ones!" and so on. We assured them that the yellow star didn't matter a bit in a blue sky and nobody saw Bobby fall down and so on, and forty very happy little girls and two exhausted leaders staggered sleepily to bed! Fifty years or more passed and I reminded the Chief Guide of that night. She remembered it perfectly and thought the Chief Scout had been there but if he was I do not remember.

About three weeks before Christmas 1912, I went back to Crowborough to settle down to a home life with parents I had seen very little of for over five years, two brothers I had hardly seen at all, and a sister-in-law I had met only when I had been a bridesmaid at her wedding. It was a strange homecoming for they all seemed to think I was the same teenager of thirteen or fourteen. The same domestic duties seemed expected of me and it was funny to be clearing the table, washing the silver, and dusting the furniture, but I soon fell into the routine and as Christmas drew near I began to get invitations from people I had known before.

CHAPTER V:

Building the Girl Guide Movement
1912–1914

The Girl Guide Association expanded rapidly. Nesta was given the task of finding a way for girls who lived far from a company to become Guides, so she started Lone Guides. Reminiscing many years later, one Guider wrote: "Lone Guiding was very thrilling; we were all 'pioneers', and many companies now large and flourishing first began as Lone efforts. The branch filled a real need for that generation of girls."

Next, Nesta persuaded her seniors to publish a magazine just for Guides. Celebrating the twenty-first birthday of The Guide, originally called the Girl Guides Gazette, Rose Kerr wrote in 1935: "what heart-searching had been gone through by the Girl Guide Executive Committee before they ventured to launch out with an 'organ' of their own! It was a great financial risk, and they realized that the paper was almost sure to be run at a loss for the first two or three years—but on the other hand, it was now absolutely necessary, if the Guide Movement were to grow and expand, for it to have its own periodical, so the great step was taken, and the first number appeared in January, 1914.

In that same twenty-first birthday issue of 1935, Lord and Lady Baden-Powell jointly signed a message which read: "How splendid to think that our own special paper, The Guide, has come of age! It has grown from such tiny, humble beginnings and has become a very important part of the Guide Movement. Thousands of readers have already been helped and inspired through its pages—may these numbers increase each year and may The Guide prove an inspiration to them all."

Nesta wrote a number of articles for the Girl Guides Gazette. An article she wrote for the first issue is reprinted in this chapter.

The year 1912 saw the end of what I might call "service in the ranks" for I went back to my home in Sussex and my friend and her parents went to live in Bournemouth where they were largely responsible for starting Guiding in that part of the country.

My father had always been an enthusiastic believer in Scouting and on my mantelpiece today there stands a bronze statuette of a Scout presented to him in 1938 by the Cubs, Scouts, and Scouters of the Crowborough District. Mother was equally in favour of Guides and gave me every encouragement in the starting of my first Company. She arranged a drawing room meeting at which Miss Agnes Baden-Powell and the Countess of Carrick spoke and as a result we were given the use of some stables as a Club Room and generous help both practical and financial. As I was well under the official age for a Captain, I was given permission to enrol my own Guides. One of the earliest members of the Company was Ada, our own housemaid, who later became housekeeper and was for many years, until her marriage, the friend and mainstay of the family. Over thirty years later Ada and I met outside the Albert Hall in London. I was supervising the loading of Extension Rangers into cars and Ada was in charge of a contingent of Rangers from Sussex. How true is the old saying "Once a Guide always a Guide!" To complete the story, Ada and her husband later moved to the same town in Hertfordshire where I was then living and we both became members of the same Trefoil Guild.

By this time, Companies were springing up like mushrooms all over Kent and Sussex and I was often asked to go and visit other Guides. One such request I remember came by telephone from Miss Macdonald who did much wonderful work as the first Headquarters Secretary. The line was very bad and all I could gather was that there were "some loose Guides near Tunbridge Wells who seemed in trouble," and before I could get more information we were cut off. Reference to a map, however, showed that there was, in fact, a village called Loose in Kent and that solved the mystery.

One morning in September 1912 I got a second phone call. Girl Guide Headquarters was receiving many requests from girls living in isolated parts of the country who longed to be Guides and could I devise a scheme by which they could be kept in touch by correspondence, that is, "Guides by Post." Miss Baden-Powell suggested they might be called "Posties" or "The Lonely Ones"! I did not like either name and I hope you agree that the word "Lones" refers to the fact that you are on your own and not in a crowd, but it certainly does not mean "lonely". With all the enthusiasm of youth, I agreed to answer letters and, in fact, to be the Captain of the first Lone Company.

A notice was put into *The Scout*, the weekly paper which most Guides received, and in no time at all letters were pouring in—thirty in the first week! I borrowed a typewriter and set to work. The letters were easy to cope with, but every would-be Guide had conscientiously worked on her Tenderfoot and Second Class Test and had sent the practical results of her labours by post.

Union Jacks appeared in every form: sewn, painted, and embroidered. Knots came tied in every variety of cord from the thinnest string to thickest rope, and pressed flowers, specimens of wood, bark, leaves, dried insects, and stones tumbled out of parcels in a bewildering heap. Most embarrassing of all, were the efforts of the girls who followed all too literally the original Scout Test "Be able to skin and cook a rabbit"! So I had rabbits boiled and rabbits roasted, and skins galore! Now, since many of these grisly relics came from Scotland and I lived in Southern England, you can imagine my family's reaction! As a matter of interest, all the rabbits were buried at the foot of a certain rose tree, which thrived well for many years on its rather peculiar fertilizer!

Many of these original Lones remained in guiding and started their own companies. Perhaps one of the best known is Marguerite de Beaumont, who wrote *The Wolf That Never Sleeps*, but there were many others who went on to reach the highest ranks of the Movement.

Referring to her Lone Guide days in the *Story of the Girl Guides*, Miss de Beaumont wrote:

> One day Miss Baden-Powell came to tea with our grandmother. She had a long talk with my sister and me, and told us about the new Movement the Chief was just starting—the Girl Guides. We were

rather horrified when she asked us to join them. We longed to be Scouts, and the Guides sounded so tame. However, she persuaded us that all the best Girl Scouts were joining so we consented. As we were not at school, and as we lived far out in the country, we became Lone Guides, and joined the first Lone company on October 12, 1912. The company had just been started, and the Captain was Miss Nesta G. Maude, Silver Fish. We never spoke of her without adding Silver Fish on to her name, because she was the first Guide in England to earn this decoration and we were immensely proud of the fact. She wrote to us only very occasionally. We got into Girl Guide uniform, instead of khaki, and we worked hard for tests and badges. Miss Maude made me Patrol Leader of the Thistle Patrol, and I corresponded with six other girls. In time I also became the proud wearer of the Silver Fish.

One historic day found me travelling with my mother and a huge hold-all to my first camp. I was deposited at Eridge Station, where the Guides met me. We tramped up a hill to camp, and then I met Miss N. G. Maude, Silver Fish, in the flesh! She was in charge of a camp of about twenty girls; we had no tents, but lived in an oast-house and slept in a loft. There were no sanitary arrangements, (Nesta always disputed this! Ed.) and we washed in one basin set on an orange box. We cooked on a fire outside, and few of us knew much about it. The programme consisted of "scouting games" and pulling a trek-cart into Eridge to fetch our own provisions. We were blissfully happy; the extreme discomfort was the nearest thing to living as pioneers and explorers. Walking back from the post-office one night I was just ahead of two people who remarked to each other: "There's one of those Girl Guides. Some people say that they are the hope of the future, the biggest thing that has happened in this country for years." My heart swelled with pride on hearing this.

Cooking

Before I left Forest Mere, Rotha and I had been asked by the Girl Guide Headquarters to organize the Girl Guide display at the Children's Welfare Exhibition to be held in January 1913 at Olympia in London. Realizing that we would no longer be living together I had refused to be officially connected with the project. I had, however, promised to spend the week in town and to be in charge of the Forest Mere Company, which was coming up to take part in the Exhibition for three days. Queen Amalie of Portugal had, from the earliest days of Guiding, been a great friend to the

Richmond Guides under Margaret Harris, and she agreed to let us camp in the empty flats over the stables. Not only did she provide us with straw for our palliasses, but also bread, milk, butter, and eggs were all ready for the girls when we arrived. The Exhibition undoubtedly was a great success and as it was the first time that Guiding had been brought before the general public it served to definitely put the Movement on the map. A great point in favour of the Guides' display was the setting of the enclosure. The floor was covered with artificial grass and in one corner was a heather-thatched shelter. In the opposite corner a little tent was pitched and the two were connected by a field telephone. Children were allowed to give a brief message to one Guide and watch while she transmitted the words by Morse code to the receiver. Cooking was carried on throughout the day on a smokeless coke fire and all sorts of little cookies, stews, stewed fruit, and custard were handed out to the audience. I only remember one unfortunate incident over a burnt stew. As chief troubleshooter I was sent for by the Manager and asked the cause of the unpleasant odour emanating from the Guides' enclosure that was pervading Olympia. Fortunately, I detected a twinkle in the eyes of a very stern face, so I replied very seriously, "Rabbit stew, sir, but the rabbit is dead and has been disposed of and we are cooking Welsh Rabbit which has a pleasant odour." Very soon after we sent a Guide to the office with a very tasty selection of cheese snacks. I wished all my peacekeeping missions had ended so pleasantly.

Mrs. Mark Kerr, in her *Story of the Girl Guides*, writes highly of the various displays and their effect on the public but admits it was accomplished at the cost of a good deal of tension. Personally, my time seemed to be spent in bus trips between Guide Headquarters and Olympia settling unpaid bills and soothing down the hurt feelings of Guide Captains or interviewing reporters and making sure that what was published was at least correct. Our Press coverage was, in fact, excellent and every morning I held a conference and gave the reporters a resume of the odd jobs that had fallen to the Guides the previous day. A story of how Rotha and I had been able to reunite a French husband and his wife who had become parted in the crowd was published in French newspapers. Guides were asked to act as escorts and messengers to the many VIPs who visited the Exhibition and many girls received souvenirs from Royal or titled patrons. I left London the evening before the Exhibition closed as I had received an invitation to make up a party for the Southdown Hunt Ball at Lewes.

Soon after this Miss Macdonald asked me if I would go and work in the Headquarters office and although, owing to home ties, I was only able to hold the job for a few months, it was an experience I shall never forget. Headquarters consisted of one room only and my duties were to sew shoulder knots, pack up uniforms, keep the petty cash book, and amuse the many visitors until such time as Miss Macdonald was at liberty to listen to their woes. When the Executive Committee was in session I did my sewing sitting on the edge of the bath, or tied up my parcels crawling about on the floor. I remember Miss Macdonald once interviewing a lady both sitting in the elevator, one of the "help yourself type" which only worked when the doors were closed. Someone, probably a Scout doing his good turn for the day, seeing the open gates, carefully closed them and at the same moment someone on the ground floor pressed the button and down went the two ladies, much to their surprise. When I was at Headquarters, one of my pet projects was ensuring that the Guides had their own weekly or monthly paper. I realized that we could never get going until there was some form of communication between the office and the people in the field. Every time there was an Executive Committee meeting I would ask Miss Macdonald, the General Secretary, if we could have a magazine of our own, and every time Miss Baden-Powell said, "We can't afford it." Finally, I tackled my journalist brother, the one who started me off by giving me *Scouting For Boys*. He worked out carefully the cost of everything and I think convinced them, because at the end of the year he was appointed editor at a microscopic salary and as a family we threw ourselves heart and soul into making the paper a success. The name was suggested by my mother who remarked one Sunday evening, "I've heard nothing but Girl Guides for two days. Tack on another 'G' and call it the Girl Guides Gazette."

1914

OUR
FIRST
EDITOR

Captain
(now Colonel)
A. H. Maude
C.M.G., D.S.O., T.D.,
D.L. County of London
(*See page* 9)

1964

GOLDEN
JUBILEE
ISSUE

Volume 51

No. 1

January
1964

Price 9d.

A Jubilee Greeting from
OUR FIRST EDITOR
Colonel A. H. Maude

**Captain Alan H Maude, First Editor of
the Girl Guides Gazette, 1914**

The first issue of the Girl Guides Gazette (January 1914) was very largely me and my brother. Alan wrote an editorial and his wife drew little sketches and was responsible for answers to correspondence. I produced an article called "How we Bridged the Duck

Pond" and in future issues wrote
on the various badges.

How We Bridged the Duck Pond

By Nesta G. Maude

(Reprinted from the January 1914 issue.)

The other day I was invited to walk across a bridge over a rainwater tank, about thirteen feet long. The bridge had been constructed by a company of Girl Guides, in about an hour, and so well did it bear that I inquired into its construction.

"Well," said the Captain, "like a good many others, I looked upon bridge-building as a thing altogether beyond my company's powers until I was struck by its fascination, and I came to the conclusion that it could be done. It is a splendid exercise for making one think and for increasing one's ingenuity.

"Our first difficulty was, of course, materials, until a friendly farmer offered us fifty or sixty good hop-poles. These are about twelve feet long, and are splendid, as 'our

ditch' is six feet deep. Rope is rather expensive stuff, but we had to lay out ten shillings in three-ply rope at a halfpenny a yard. This we cut into three-yard lashings, and all the ends were neatly finished with a crown knot and three tucks.

"Of course, this was not nearly enough cord, but my clever Lieutenant, there, was seized with an inspiration, and as a result of it we paid a visit to our farmer friend, and asked what happened to the hop-string after the hops were picked. He told us it was all cut up and left in those bundles one sees in the hop-gardens.

"We went down and collected any quantity, some old and rotten, but some almost quite new, and quite strong enough to lash parts where there is not much strain, as, for instance, the diagonals.

"There were our materials, and we decided to make our first bridge the same as the one you see here, a four-legged trestle bridge. We made one trestle and launched it, but, to our dismay, it would not settle, but kept bobbing about. It obviously wanted weighting, and we solved the difficulty by slinging two drain-pipes on to the fork of the diagonals."

"But how did you learn all that you know?" I asked.

"Read it up," replied the Captain. "I got the 'Manual of Field Engineering,' and also Part III of Military Engineering. The butcher gave me hickory skewers, and I made models till I understood the principle of trestle bridges. Then I took to visiting ponds and streams in the neighbourhood, and thinking out ways of bridging them. One need not always have water, a sunk lane or hollow in a field will give excellent practice."

It all sounded quite easy, and I determined my Company should start at once to learn Pioneering; so I asked my friend if she could not bicycle over and give us some instruction. She was delighted, and we arranged that she should bring over two of her best girls the next Saturday, and in the meantime I should try and get fifty good hop-poles. They offered to bring lashings. Before leaving, I took a photograph of the whole Company on its bridge.

Next Saturday turned out a lovely day, and my Company paraded at 2:00 p.m., in full strength (twenty-two). We had decided to bridge a little duck pond, and when the Captain and her girls arrived we showed them our choice.

"Very good," said she, "but first of all I must make you all sit down and listen to a few facts and figures!"

So down we all squatted!

"Now," went on our instructor, "so far as we are concerned there are only two sorts of bridges, trestle and floating. There are others, but they are beyond our capabilities. In fact, all I am interested in now are trestle bridges—that is, a series of two, three or four-legged trestles connected by the roadway. The space between the trestles is a 'bay' and their length depends on the strength of your material.

"Now, what do you think is the first thing to be done before starting to bridge?"

Someone suggested getting someone over to the other side! But this was quite impossible for we had to imagine that our pond was a slow-running river, with low banks and no ford for miles either side of us!

"Find out how deep it is!" shouted No. 3 of the Cornflowers, and we all thought how silly we were not to think of that before.

"That's right," said the Captain, "and also find out what sort of bottom it is. If it is muddy, the horizontal bars of the trestles (called ledgers) should be lashed quite near the bottom; if it is rocky, they should be quite high up."

We found the depth by lashing one pole, or "spar," as we were told to call them, at right angles to the tip of another, and prodding the bottom as far as the Captain's long arms could reach.

"Eight feet and a soft bottom," was the verdict. "Now we are going to build a two-legged trestle bridge which will allow people to pass over in single file."

The girls were then divided into squads of six, and three lots started to make trestles under supervision. First, they laid two spars, very stout ones, parallel to each other, about four feet apart, and the Captain pushed the tips about two inches nearer to each other. These were the legs, and the depth of the water was carefully marked on them with a piece of chalk.

"Now lash the transoms, that is, the spar on which the roadway will rest."

One girl wanted to put it on the water mark, but she was shown that that would make the roadway touch the water, so the transom went about one foot from the water-line. Being a muddy bottom, the ledgers went about three feet from the "butts" (thick ends) of the legs, on the same sides as the transoms. Then came the diagonals or braces, as they are called. They were put on with both tips and one butt on the opposite side of the leg to the transoms and ledger, and the other butt on the same side. Now the trestle looked like this:

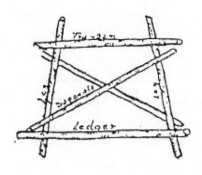

Trestle

In the meantime, two sturdy Guides had been hammering in two stakes, about four and a half feet high, at the water's edge, as "pickets." The first trestle was fixed only a few feet away, and, as the water was shallow, the legs had to be shortened a little. Two spars were lashed from the tops of the pickets to the tops of the legs.

"Now lay three stout spars from the shore to the transom," said the Captain. "These are the road bearers. The shore ends can be made firm with stones and earth, and you must lash the others to the transom with one long lashing, taking two turns round road bearer and transom. Next, lay on your planks—'chesses' is the proper name. These go across the width of the bridge, and are kept firm by spars laid along the edges, and lashed at intervals to the two outside road bearers. These spars are called 'ribands.' A good substitute for chesses are Guides' staffs, lashed about six inches apart."

Now, everyone was summoned to see the second trestle launched.

First, two spars were laid from the first transom down into the water. Two long cords were slipped round the legs of No. 2, below the ledger, and tied with a long bowline, so that the knot could be reached to be untied. A strong Patrol Leader now took the trestle and held it above her head, and stepped on to the transom of No. 1. She put the ledger of No. 2 on to the 'ways' and let it slide. The two Guides who held the cords regulated its pace, and when the Leader felt its legs touch the bottom she called "Steady!" and, taking a light spar from another Guide, she lashed it at right angles to the top of one leg. Then she did the same with another one, and by working these handrails trestle No. 2 was soon in position, about four feet from No. 1.

The handrails were made fast to the legs of the first trestle, and then the Captain began to talk of "cross-bracings."

She said that the person who undertook these had to perform extraordinary gymnastic feats. She then explained that the legs of all the trestles had to be connected by two spars, going from just under the transom on one leg to as low down as possible on the next, and fixed with a diagonal lashing where they crossed.

By the time this was done, other Guides had made the roadway to the second trestle, and No. 3 was waiting.

Out went the 'ways' again, and No. 3 slid into position. Handrails were fixed as before, and the same work went on till our bridge began to look quite professional.

One of my company said she "did not seem to realize she was working over eight feet of water," and another said she "should never be content again with lashings that were 'fairly firm,' because she saw how important it was for every Guide to do her job as near perfectly as she could."

Now we all knew our work, we got on splendidly, and at about 4:30 the last Guide had passed over in safety, and we raised a proper Guides cheer for our visitor, who had taught us so much. For what we had learned may be put to very practical use in repairing broken bridges over streams or ditches, or in cases of bridges destroyed by fire or flood.

"If the trestle will not stand firm," said the Captain, "weight it with sacks of stones or sand. Remember always to limit the number of people crossing to 'one person to a bay,' and if your bridge is left unguarded, put up a notice to that effect on both ends.

"If your material is weak, common sense would tell you to double such important parts as the legs and transoms."

As we sat round the camp fire and drank our tea, the Captain told us some proper yarns of a Lone Patrol she knew, but I have neither time nor space to pass them on to you, so, as the books say, "we must close."

The Bridge, 1913-1914

The magazine caught on wonderfully and before the year was out, at tuppence a month, it was more than paying its way. In July my brother, a member of the Territorial Army, took with him to army camp the proofs of the September issue of the *Girl Guides Gazette*, which included a serial by a very well known writer of the day. The papers were all in a dispatch case, which was stolen when he was suddenly recalled to the War Office. We were all sure it was taken by a foreign agent who, no doubt, thought he was obtaining top-secret documents. We hoped he enjoyed the adventures of "Pat of the Poppy Patrol."

Early in June 1914, Sussex held its first County Rally at which both the Chief and his sister were present. As I had a good deal to do with the arrangements, I was delighted at the way it went off. When the official party entered the field there was not a Scout or Guide to be seen but at a given signal they rushed out from behind a belt of trees coming to a smart halt in a horseshoe facing the piled drums of the 5th Battalion of the Royal Sussex Regiment. On the drums were draped two flags, the Scouts' flag given by my father, and the Guides' flag, a gift from my mother, and these were duly dedicated by the Bishop of Lewes. Unfortunately, my mother was not well enough to attend the Rally and a week later the two flags, draped in black, were carried to her funeral when Scouts and Guides lined the little country churchyard in which she was laid to rest.

Two months later my father and I were on our way to Norway. Our luggage was actually on the boat when a telegram from my brother advised our returning to London immediately, and that day war was declared.

The only record of any active Guide work on my part during the war years is contained in the Chief Guide's diary for 1916. In it she refers to a meeting of Commissioners for Sussex and as I happened to be on leave at the time, I was asked to attend. My embarrassment at finding that half the ladies present bore a title and that I was considerably the youngest of the company may be imagined, and when I was asked to speak about the practical training I nearly bolted out of the room. Lady Baden-Powell soon put me at my ease by saying quietly, "Just pretend we are a lot of new girls and tell us the things we shall learn and why they will be useful to us." Once started, I found it easy to explain to a Duchess that fire-lighting, tracking, and observation were all good training in concentration and the ability to tie a bowline or a knot that would not slip might one day lead to the saving of a life.

CHAPTER VI:

The First World War
1914–1919

During the First World War women were given opportunities to serve their country in ways that had previously been the prerogative of men. The Women's Land Army was formed, which took over farm labouring jobs to free men for the trenches in France. In 1916 the youngest of the three armed forces, the Royal Flying Corps, recruited women to drive its motor transport.

As Nesta loved anything mechanical, she joined the Women's Land Army early in the war, but when the Royal Flying Corps opened its doors to women she quickly transferred. She was demobilized on September 20, 1919, and in her demobilization booklet an officer wrote: "A very capable trustworthy driver."

On June 6, 1914, my mother died after a very brief illness and six weeks later my father and I were on our way to Norway having let our Sussex house for four months. We spent a few nights with cousins in Leeds but our heavy luggage went straight on board the boat in Hull. My eldest brother was in camp with his Territorial unit. On August 3 my father received a telegram from him, "Strongly advise return London immediately." As my brother was of the "unflappable" kind, we took his advice and travelled south in a train packed with reservists rejoining their units in a spirit of hilarity, in some cases activated by recourse to a bottle. My youngest brother had managed to get rooms for us in the house in which he lodged in the Marylebone Road, but no sooner was I in bed the first night than my brother poked his head round the door and said, "There's a hairy old fire quite close—come on." I threw on some clothes and ran down the stairs to find my father, perfectly turned out and carrying his suitcase! He had misunderstood my brother's remark and thought it referred to "Heavy firing quite close," and he was quite prepared to carry out any orders given by the authorities! Having assured him he was quite free to return to bed, my brother and I ran down the road to watch a most spectacular fire in a garage.

Next day, my two brothers and their Territorial unit were confined to barracks in the Duke of York's Headquarters and Father and I were kept busy. Every morning we would collect lists of requirements from officers of various ranks. A typical day's shopping might be something like this: four dozen large khaki handkerchiefs, holster for service revolver, pair of spurs, six shirts, twelve pairs of socks (assorted sizes), sword and scabbard, tooth paste, and finally, "Take back mess jacket to tailor for alteration"!

By October we were able to move back to Sussex, but our luggage, which had sailed away to Norway, did not turn up for another month. Back home in Crowborough we found a huge hutment camp in the process of erection and there were rumours of thousands of troops expected any time. My father realized at once that a canteen must be set up in the village to afford some sort of relaxation for the soldiers. There was only one hall of any sort available and this was taken over by a small committee which my father soon got together. He then proceeded, in the most reckless fashion, to order tables, chairs, crockery, and urns while an army of willing helpers scrubbed, cleaned, and decorated the dirty old hall. A week before the troops were due my father went to London and arranged with his old firm, National Bakeries, to send daily by train large slabs of cake and tins of biscuits. Having done all this he went to the YMCA and offered Sir Arthur Yapp a fully equipped canteen, together with a detailed account of all the money he had spent, less the generous donations made by the local people. I do not think the YMCA hesitated a moment over these accounts but when my father realized that the total was just 5 shillings short of a good round sum he said very quickly that he had forgotten to add the cost of a bread slicer, which of course was necessary!

During this time I certainly was not idle. While we were in London I had gone back to the Girl Guide office and was loaned to the Boy Scouts to help with the selection of boys to replace the Coastguards. After interviewing one fifteen year old, I asked how soon he could arrange to move. A glance at his watch and the answer came, "Ten minutes if I might use your phone to let my mother know I shan't be in to supper." No wonder the Chief was proud of his boys. I had also volunteered—and had been accepted—for a unit being organized by Mrs. Sinclair Stobart who had served in the Balkan War as head of the First Aid Nursing Yeomanry. A few days before we were due to leave, however, the Germans had entered Brussels and before the unit was reorganized it was discovered that I was under the minimum age and therefore ineligible.

Early in 1915, my father was asked to organize the large YMCA Canteen at Seaford Camp. In order to be on the spot we moved to a little cottage on the Downs. The first Sunday we walked over to Cuckmere Haven and found Scouts in charge of the Coastguard duties. I remember they were having a small problem with their Sunday dinner and although no cook I was able to be of some help, and before we left arrangements had been made for the two boys off duty on Sunday mornings to walk over to our cottage and collect a good, hot meal. Our dear old cook, Edith, loved to prepare hearty meals and I can see her now adding vegetables and dumplings to a stew and saying, "They're big, growing boys. Bless 'em." They were also allowed to bring a limited amount of heavy laundry and any mending they were unable to cope with themselves.

Soon after we returned home, one of my father's sisters asked if she might come and live with us, and I was free to look for the war work I knew was waiting somewhere just for me. My wonderful Lieutenant, being a teacher, would not be moved and was ready and willing to take over the Crowborough Guides, and they are mentioned in the *Girl Guides Gazette* as doing valiant war service. A Guide friend of many years had been asked if she would work on a farm as part of an experiment to see to what extent girls could take the place of men on the land. She agreed, on condition I could go with her, and so we found ourselves working for Roland Marsh in the village of Hawkedon, Suffolk. The first idea was to see if we could drive the International Harvester Tractors, huge heavy machines, very different to the light combines of present day use. Behind them they pulled a plough on which was seated some one who regulated the depth of the furrow. If by chance the front share struck a rock, the rider was most likely to be unseated and to end up rolling on the ground. The starting up of these monsters was far beyond the strength of most girls. When cold, first thing in the morning, it was fairly easy, and a hard pull on the flywheel would be enough to start the motor firing but once the engine got hot and it became necessary to switch off, it was indeed a major effort to get it started again. Personally, I was soon able to cope competently with the tractor and fairly well with the plough, but I had to point out to

Mr. Marsh I was physically tougher and stronger than most girls and I doubted if many others would stand up to a sixty-hour week of such hard labour.

My friend left after a month and I moved into the foreman's house as a lodger, and pretty soon I was replacing the lorry drivers while they moved onto tractors, and this arrangement seemed to suit everyone concerned. I usually drove a three-tonne Daimler truck carting corn, hay, and straw to the Army Remount Depot at Sudbury and picking up loads of coal for the steam engines and barrels of tar and granite chips for the County Council. My mate, Bert, was a delightful youngster who took more than his fair share of the heavy work and never grumbled. Like many arable farmers Marsh refused to change to Daylight Saving Time with the result that we worked by "God's Time," but trains, posts, and the church followed Government Time. The first day of the changeover Bert and I drove into the yard, delighted at the prospect of another hour of daylight and with a plan for going into Bury St. Edmunds on Bert's motor bike, but as we were quietly fading away the office door burst open and the Boss demanded to know "where we thought we were off to with the sun so high in the heavens?"

I was paid 24 shillings a week of which 14 shillings went for board and lodging and added to this was an average of 3 to 4 shillings for overtime at fourpence an hour. Hours were 6:00 a.m. to 6:00 p.m. and half day Saturday. The men accepted me for what I was, just another worker, and I soon acquired a rich Suffolk accent with all the colloquialisms and swear words necessary to carry on a conversation with the average farm labourer of those days. It was a hard life but I enjoyed it and sometimes I had some interesting breaks. Once, the Boss took over a holding that had been so badly farmed that the War Agricultural Committee was only too happy to let it to him for a very nominal sum. The first thing was to rid the property of rabbits and Charlie, the rabbit catcher, and I would start off at 5:00 a.m. in the little Darraque with our sack of ferrets, two guns, and dogs. I wore out the knees of two pairs of breeches kneeling by rabbit holes waiting for the occupants to be bolted by our ferrets. In the evening we packed the day's catch off to London by train.

Another time I spent two weeks in the woods near Hadleigh. My job (assistant to Sugar Martin, our horse keeper) was to lead my horse into the wood, hitch him to a newly felled tree, and haul the log to the saw bench. We started work on a Monday and by midday I was very grateful for two things: first, that I was a Girl Guide, and secondly, that it was a Monday! It was the custom then for us to carry our dinner and snacks in white linen bags like shoe bags. These were then put into an American cloth bag with a drawstring and this could be hung on a bicycle or the lamp of a car or the hames of a horse collar and were far easier to carry than baskets or tins. This morning one of the younger men lost three fingers in the saw, and with about twenty spotlessly clean white bags to call on we were able to pad the stumps and I drove the lad to the nearest hospital. As well as our lunches, usually the crusty top of a cottage loaf with a little hollow filled with butter, cheese, and onion, our bags also contained a mid-morning snack and one for mid-afternoon. These five-minute breaks were known as "Beaver" and "Mitten" but I have quite forgotten which was which and as I never saw the words in print I have no idea how they were spelled.

One of the first things I learned to do at the farm was to ride a motorbike. Marsh had bought it thinking he would get around the farms a bit quicker, but he fell off it so often he decided in favour of a second car. The bike in question was a huge thing. I was told it was a seven horsepower Zenith, but to me it was "The Monster." One of the men who had a bike of his own showed me how to run and leap into the saddle, but I had only wobbled uncertainly round the yard a couple of times when the very next morning, while it was still dark, I was awakened by stones thrown at the window and the Boss asking—or rather telling—me to get on the Zenith and go to Bury St. Edmunds and collect a draught for the cow.

I remember telling myself as I got dressed that I would get to Bury on "The Monster" even if I had to push it up the hills and coast down them! As a matter of fact, that early morning ride laid the foundation of a firm friendship between me and "The Monster" that lasted for one and a half years.

I shall never forget my first harvest. Is the harvest in Suffolk still "sold," I wonder? In my time the Boss and his labourers would come to an agreement by which the farmer would pay each man a lump sum and the men agreed to work all hours and no overtime.

In 1915, all had gone well. The last load but one was at the stack and I was toiling up the hill with my loaded waggon and two horses, the wheeler and the leader. This job is known as "driving away," which is probably a corruption of driving a "wain," as in Suffolk a waggon is frequently called a wain. As we approached the gate into the stack yard, my leader, tired, no doubt (as we all were), stumbled—the wheeler swerved and the waggon wheel hit the gate post and over went the wain and its load of wheat and all the hopes of an early finish!

I remember thinking of something I had learned as a Girl Guide, "if a horse falls down, sit on its head." I had no chance to practice my knowledge, for Sugar Martin, our horse keeper, leaped off the stack and said two words to old Boxer who lay still.

Sugar said a lot more words to me, most of them unprintable here. After I had weeded out the uncomplimentary ones, I knew I had to take both horses to the pond and water them, and that back in the stable I was to unharness them, hang up the gear, rub Boxer and Rosie down well, feed them, and bed them down. By this time the fallen sheaves were all on the stack and the tarpaulin was in place.

The men had gone home to tea and a wash up before gathering in the little pub for the customary end-of-harvest jollification. When I told my landlady what had happened and that I wasn't going out, she and her husband laughed and said, "Go and have a good booze. It'll do you good!" So after a wash and a clean shirt I went, to be greeted with laughter and tales of previous harvests in which it appeared that nearly everyone in the smoke-filled pub had, at some time, overturned a wain.

So life went on for a year and a half and had it not been for a parcel of kippers I might well have finished the war in Suffolk! One afternoon I was sent to Bury St. Edmunds to cash the weekly wage cheque and, as usual, I bought as many kippers as I could collect at the request of the men's wives. The parcel was wrapped in a London newspaper and my eye fell on a paragraph to the effect that the Royal Flying Corps was recruiting girls to replace men in the cookhouse and mechanical transport. I was always fascinated by engines, and some of my happiest hours on the farm were spent as "mate" to Charlie Orbell, our mechanic, who repaired all the cars, lorries, and tractors. If we were working late the Boss would call us into the office for supper. Frequently, this would consist of a huge Spanish onion in white sauce and a mug of hot, sweet, milky cocoa. An odd sort of meal? Maybe, but how good it was at 9:00 p.m. on a cold winter night.

Having made up my mind to try for the Royal Flying Corps the next thing was to get a day off, for the cutting said "Apply in person only" at Devonshire House, London. As it turned out, I did not even have to ask for time off as the Boss wanted a load of chaff taken to London and some heavy spare parts for the tractors brought back. I set out in my working clothes, breeches, khaki shirt, sweater, and neck scarf to prevent chaff falling down my neck, but in a parcel in the toolbox was a respectable coat and skirt and nice shoes and stockings. I delivered the chaff and left the lorry to be loaded, agreeing to pick it up about four o'clock. After changing in the Ladies' Room in Liverpool Street Station, I made my way to Green Park Station and across the road to Devonshire House. I was interviewed by a Major who asked me three questions. First: was I strong and healthy? Second: What types and makes of cars had I driven, and for how long? (After the first ten names he stopped me and said he would get a motor catalogue for the rest!) And third: Could I report to the Central Flying School at Upavon on Salisbury Plain the next day? I was terrified that if I said "no" I should lose my chance of being posted to what sounded like a wonderful station. However, I had to explain that as I was paid weekly and had been with my present employer a year and a half I could not in fairness leave without a week's notice. The Major agreed and said as Central Flying School had been short of drivers for weeks he guessed they could wait a bit longer. He explained that at some stations girls did not drive after dark and were employed only on Fords and Staff Cars, but at Central Flying school he thought they drove everything and was sure I would fit in well with the present group of girls.

I must have driven home safely but I was still walking on air when I went into the office to confess what I had done. The fates were certainly on my side that day for the Boss had just heard of a Belgian refugee who had worked for him before was at liberty to come back. Mr. Marsh said he would certainly not have sacked me and was sorry to see me go but under the circumstances would not exercise his right and refuse to release me. So in a couple of days I was ready to leave. I travelled to London with three friends, two soldiers rejoining their units after leave and a girl who was in the theatrical world. Among my belongings was a little, old-fashioned gramophone, and as we had the compartment to ourselves at the beginning of the journey, we all became rather hilarious playing with the horn of the instrument, making noises down it and using it as an ear trumpet. Somewhere on the journey a little old lady got in and dropped her glove. One of the boys picked it up and made some polite remark which he was asked to repeat, and then to our horror the lady produced from her reticule an ear trumpet, a minia-ture of the horn we had been fooling with. I think I joined the boys in the corridor leaving the actress to cope with the situation, which she did without the flicker of a smile.

We were all staying that night at the Bonnington Hotel in the Strand and had taken tickets for Chu Chin Chow, then at the height of its popularity. Soon after the curtain went up there was an air raid warning and the stage manager gave the usual warning. We could either wait for the "all clear" when the play would be resumed, or leave the theatre. We stayed. At the end of the performance we decided to walk to the hotel but before we got there we found bar-riers up and were told the hotel had been bombed. I have only a vague idea of the amount of damage done, but I know my luggage was unharmed and I imagine alternative accommodation was found for us. The next morning I collected my railway warrant from Paddington to Pewsey and set off to start a new life in the Royal Flying Corps.

I was met at Pewsey by a tall, fair girl with a motorcycle and a sidecar and during the seven mile drive to the Central Flying School, which stood on the downs at the top of a hill leading out of the little village of Upavon, she pointed out many features of the countryside. Just across the River Avon stood another aerodrome called Netheravon, and I learned that there was bitter rivalry between the two stations in practically all departments, but especially in the Transport Section. I gathered that girls posted to Netheravon were not allowed to do Flying Duty and had to hand their vehicles over to men drivers for night duty. I was also told that unless I wanted to be stuck on Fords for the duration I had better say firmly that I couldn't drive one. Our Ford van drivers did seem to have dull lives compared to the drivers of Crossley tenders. Their duties were chiefly confined to Camp, coffee rounds, driving the Padre or Medical Officer on their visits, and meeting new officers at various stations.

Central Flying School was, of course, my first experience of a military aerodrome, or in fact of any aerodrome, to say nothing of the rows of stone-built quarters and huge hangers, which filled me with excitement and the hope that I should pass all my tests and be accepted into this wonderful world. I also learned that women cooks and transport drivers were all members of the Women's Legion but we seemed to come under ordinary discipline and to be subject to the King's Regulations.

Arriving at the Transport Yard, I was handed over to Sergeant-Major Jackson who led me out to a Crossley Tender and waved me into the driver's seat. When I first learned to drive in 1908 I was taught three basic rules to follow before attempting to start any engine. First, walk round the car to see that all tires were as they should be; second, make sure the car was in neutral and the brake on; and third, grasp the starting handle with the thumb on the same side as the fingers. This last precaution, if followed, would have prevented many a broken or sprained wrist occurring as the result of a backfire. This ritual obviously pleased the Sergeant-Major and I knew I had come through the first driving test, but when an eleven-foot trailer was hitched on to the tender I began to feel a bit apprehensive as to my ability to cope with this lengthy appendage. I had pulled harrows and hay rakes with our little Darraque on the farm so I had a rough idea of the technique necessary to reverse a trailer. Even so, it took me three tries before I put the trailer neatly between the others on the parking lot. I was sent off then to get my dinner.

Our mess hut was next door to the cook house so our meals were always hot, and the hut contained some comfortable chairs and a piano which the girls rented themselves. Next door were our sleeping quarters, originally the Sergeants' block. They consisted of about twelve double-sided cubicles and four baths and were heated by an open fireplace at each end of the block. The other girls were all friendly and ready to answer all my questions but when I said my surname was Maude they laughed and said I would have to change that. They were all called by their second names, except in the case of the two Bulteel sisters, one of whom was known as Bull and her sister as Bullet. My name was soon settled when it was found that I possessed a long, thick khaki scarf which Bullet said made me look like Old Bill, one of the then popular Bairnsfather cartoons. Bill I was christened, and Bill I have remained to those of my co-drivers with whom I still correspond.

After lunch I had a short trip on a thirty cwt. Leyland and was told to change a tire on a Crossley wheel. A few questions about driving in general and reading a map and it was all over and I was entitled to a khaki uniform with the black and white shoulder flashes of the Royal Flying Corps. I was then sent off with one of the Ford drivers on a tour of the station and I learned the position of the main buildings—Guard room, Orderly Room, Officers' Mess, hospital, YMCA, workshops, squadron hangers and so on—but I was also well drilled in the duties of Crash Tender Driver.

The Crash Driver and Ambulance Driver stood out on the aerodrome with a powerful pair of binoculars watching every plane in the air. The minute a plane appeared to be in difficulties we concentrated on it and if a crash seemed inevitable we flung the glasses to our relief driver and tore to our car. Orders were to proceed to the hospital blowing the horn in a series of blasts—toot, toot, toot. This ensured clear roads and was also a warning to Mutt and Jeff, our medical orderlies, to be ready. They would be waiting with two baskets of equipment and a bottle of some liquid, which we were told would explode if we braked suddenly or bumped over a rough patch. Nobody ever told us what this bottle contained and nobody took the tale very seriously. Our job was to get to the crash as fast as possible. The downs in that part of Wiltshire run in ridges, rather like corrugated cardboard, and we were told to keep to the top of the ridge until we could see the crash and then use our own discretion as to the best way to reach it. Sometimes another pilot in the air would have seen the accident and he would circle and dive and waggle his wings to draw our attention to the spot. The Ambulance, usually driven by "Shady" Lane, would follow us, but even with three men it was not unusual for the Crash Driver to be brought in to help get the pilot out from the tangled wreckage or to help with the stretcher. In my time, there was a curious tradition at Central Flying School. If the pilot was alive he was lifted into the Ambulance, but if he had been killed outright, the body was placed in the crash tender. The length of these vehicles must have been about five and a half feet with the result that in the case of a tall man, the feet would show under the drawn back curtain. This indicated to everyone that the crash had been fatal and gave rise to the wildest speculation as to who the casualty was. The first crash I attended was not serious, a broken nose, facial cuts, and crushed ribs. When I got back the Sergeant-Major asked how I had got on and said that if I felt I could not stand up to that sort of thing I could be excused. Actually, I only remember one girl taking advantage of this offer, and she was soon transferred at her own request to the Royal Army Service Corps on staff cars.

A few days later and before I was even in uniform I was detailed to take a trailer to Chichester to collect a crashed plane. I remember that soon after leaving the school we had a puncture, but the Flight Sergeant and Air Mechanic with me soon changed the wheel and we carried on. At Chichester we found the pilot and his Flight Commander, who had flown over, staying at the best hotel. They were very surprised to find a civilian driver but it was a great break for me as Taffy Jones, the Flight commander, taught me everything a Mechanical Transport Driver should know if sent to a forced landing which necessitated an overnight stop. I learned that on the road the driver was in charge and was responsible for choosing the route and finding the plane, but once the machine was located the Flight Sergeant or senior "Ack Emma" (Air Mechanic) took over and the driver carried out his instructions as to the positioning of the tender and trailer. If, as often happened, the forced landing was in an isolated spot, we had to use our own discretion, find some respectable lodging, or go to the nearest police station. I spent a very comfortable night once on the floor of the police station at Cosham. I also discovered that if on a long trip a "comfort halt" became necessary, the unwritten law was "ladies to the right" and "gentlemen to the left."

Next day the crashed machine was loaded on the trailer and we had an excellent run back. I received two very minor reprimands after this trip. The first, that as the puncture had occurred within ten miles of Central Flying school, I should really have returned either to pick up another spare wheel or hand over to another driver and tender; secondly, I put on my duty sheet that I had collected a "Pup", and this, it appeared, was only a slang term and that I had really collected a "Sopwith." Both these errors were put down to inexperience and I seemed to have come through my first forced landing pretty well. Detailing was all in the hands of the detailing sergeants and I think Brattle, Freddy, Gibby, and Wilkie (the names by which we knew them) did their job very fairly. Anyone who had finished a tough week of flying duty was pretty sure to be given a nice run with one or two nights out the following week. If, on the other hand, they had grumbled, not kept the brass polished on their car, or shown a poor petrol average, it might mean three or four days of Camp roads, carting furniture, or taking bedding to be cleaned. On the whole though, I think we all took the rough with the smooth and remained a pretty harmonious group of girls.

Three incidents I shall always remember. It had never occurred to me that there would be a chance of flying, but on one occasion I had taken a Flight Sergeant out to a forced landing, but when the Flight Commander arrived in a two-seater Avro it was decided that the Sergeant should be left to dismantle the engine while the Flight Commander flew back for some spare parts, taking me with him to carry the bits and pieces. Later on I had quite a few flips (short flights) with an instructor. On another occasion I had spent two nights at Kintbery while a mechanic fitted a new engine. When the time came to start up I was called on to help pull on the propeller, but with no result. Finally, the pilot suggested that I should sit in the plane while he added his strength to that of the Air Mechanic. "Just rev her up gently," were my instructions, but to my horror the plane jumped the wheel chocks and headed for the hedge. I had enough presence of mind to keep the tail down while I switched off the engine and brought the plane to a standstill. I thought I had managed pretty well and was not at all prepared for the blast I got for switching off and giving the men the trouble of starting the engine again. The second time, fortunately, all went well, and that evening I received a box of a hundred cigarettes from the pilot.

Nesta Maude Ashworth

Central Flying School Upavon, Wilts.

"If Our Friends Could See Us Now!"

"I'm on staff!" C.O.s car and driver

A different working style

Crossley Crash Tender, 1917

6001 getting a wash

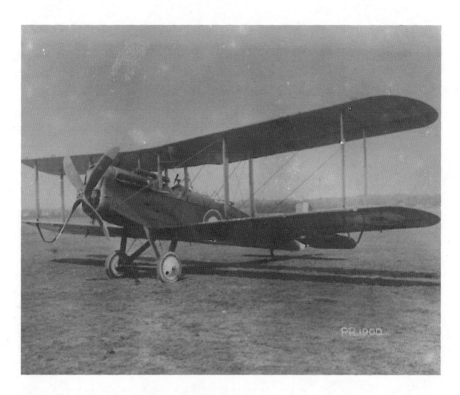

My third memory, although it gave me some bad moments at the time, is perhaps the most pleasant of all. I was detailed to take the Commandant's car to Ludgershall Station to meet three senior officers. No names were given but I was told to be sure and take the C.O.'s fur rug and "see your buttons are clean," and by this I gathered the Brass Hats were pretty high up. One of them, General Brancker, I had driven before and he greeted me with "Morning, Bill" as the three entered the car, and I spread the rug over their knees. It so happened that for some reason no coal had been delivered to the school for a week and like everyone else we Mechanical Transport girls were suffering from the cold in our sleeping quarters and no hot baths. On the way back from the station I was puzzling over the identity of the youngest of the three officers, but I couldn't place him. Suddenly, in the middle of the road, I saw a huge lump of coal, evidently fallen off a load. I knew I ought to drive round it but, after all, it meant possibly three or four warm evenings, a hot drink at night, and at least enough warm water to brush our teeth in. I thought I could easily jump out and lift the black diamond onto the floor beside me but I soon found I couldn't even move it. By that time it was a case of "might as well be hung for a sheep as a lamb," and I began to tip the lump over and over till one end rested on the running board, and with a final tremendous heave I got my prize in the car, and with scarlet cheeks I leapt over the spare wheel and we sped on. My heart sank when I saw the guard had been turned out and the Commandant and Adjutant were waiting on the Orderly Room steps to greet my passengers. I jumped out, opened the door, took the rug and gave what I hoped was my snappiest salute. General Brancker got out first saying, "Thanks, Bill." The older officer came next with a smile and "Thank you." Then came the youngest officer who said with a slight stammer, "I hope you enjoy a nice fire tonight!" Then he preceded the other two officers into the orderly room and I was left staggered at what I had done to H.R.H. The Duke of York, later King George VI! For the rest of the day I went about miserably wondering what would happen to me—seven days confined to barracks, loss of my stripes or, worst of all, grounded and forbidden to drive for a week. I need not have worried. I never heard a word, and the Adjutant said all my officers were full of admiration for my action and rather ashamed that they had not offered to help, but after all they could hardly appear with coal streaked hands and possibly black marks on their new blue uniforms!

It must not be thought that life in the Royal Flying Corps was all work. To me, at first, it seemed like a rest cure, but we were on duty from 8:30 a.m. to 6:00 p.m. The Crash Driver was awakened at crack of dawn by the Duty Corporal, who entered our quarters and shook the sleepy girl to the accompaniment of "Come on Bill, show a leg" or "Bullet, if you don't wake up, I'll douse you!" Still only half awake, the driver would hustle into her uniform and trot over to the Transport Yard and start up her tender. Often in the winter it was necessary to get a Leyland out to tow the Crossleys in order to start them. Once the crash tender and ambulances were in position and flying had started, a Ford Van would come round with tea, hot, black and sweet, and I always felt if that witches' brew did not wake one up, nothing would! The Crash Driver or her relief remained on duty until all the squadrons reported they were closing down. Then the car had to be checked to make sure it was fit for service the next day. We were supposed to have Saturday afternoons and all day Sunday off, but in the early days there were so few of us that by the time one had eliminated the Duty Driver, Crash, Ford, Crossley, and staff and allowed for one or two vehicles out on forced landings there were often only one or two girls able to take advantage of these "Off days." Several girls played the piano and we used to sing and dance in our mess hut. Many of the officers ran their own small cars and, provided a girl was not a Duty Driver, she was free to go out with the escort of her choice, so long as she was in for roll call at 10:00 p.m.

In January 1918, rumours began to circulate about the proposed amalgamation of the Royal Flying Corps and the Royal Naval Air Service. The one that seemed to affect us most was the formation of the Women's Royal Air Force. When I first went to Central Flying School the drivers were in the charge of a South African girl called Larsen, but after a few months she was posted and the job was offered to me, and although I was junior in length of service to some of the girls, it seemed to be their choice and I accepted on one condition. This was that, unlike Larsen who never drove, I should continue as an active Crossley driver, and instead of being called Head Driver I became Sergeant with three stripes. We were all given the choice of joining the new Women's Royal Air Force and remaining with aeroplanes or transferring to the Royal Army Service Corps. A few girls took the latter alternative but most of the old hands stuck to Central Flying School, and when we were told that we could wear our khaki uniforms and flashes as long as they lasted we all immediately sent off orders to Selfridges for a replacement of the uniforms of which we had become so proud.

At first it seemed as if the formation of the Women's Royal Air Force was going to make a big difference to our social life. One of the first orders forbade officers and other ranks from being seen together in public. It had always been the custom for an officer, the M.T. Driver and the Air Mechanic to feed together in any pub, restaurant, or hotel that was handy to the forced landing or crash on which they happened to be working. Among other things bound to be affected were the weekly dances held in one of the hangars and attended by all ranks. The number of women on the station had been greatly increased by the arrival of members of Queen Mary's Army Auxiliary Corps who were working as clerks in the Orderly Room and waitresses in the Officer's Mess. Naturally these dances were very popular and it was quite usual to see the Assistant Commandant or the Adjutant dancing with one of the Orderly Room staff or a waitress. We Transport girls by reason of our employment naturally found our friends among the Squadron and Flying Officers. As the first Saturday after the Anti-Social order was issued approached we all wondered what would happen. I was a bit late getting to the hangar but the dance floor seemed as full as usual. The faces, too, seemed familiar. I could see the Transport Officer dancing with one of his clerks but he appeared to have been demoted from Captain to Flight Sergeant. There was in fact not an officer's tunic to be seen. Soon after this I was in London with our equipment officer and as we had to wait until the next day for some parts we decided to go to the "Bing Boys." We carefully scanned the audience for the sight of an RAF brass hat and not seeing one we took our seats and thoroughly enjoyed the show. A few days later I was driving an officer from another station and he asked casually how I had liked the "Bing Boys." It transpired that he was also escorting a girl of other rank.

About this time I was sent for by the Commandant and asked if I would consider taking a commission and being in charge of all technical WRAF drivers and workshop personnel. I cannot imagine what induced me to agree to letting my name go forward. I never liked office or administration work and after driving motor vehicles for over ten years I should have known I ought to have said "no"! I tried to comfort myself by saying the war would be over in a few months and the extra pay and gratuity would be a great help in the future. A month later the C.O. hailed me from the top of the Orderly Room steps with the words, "Oh, Bill, I've cancelled your commission, told 'em you weren't suitable." As at least a dozen officers must have heard this remark my first reaction was one of disgust at thus being labelled inefficient, but the Old Man went on, "They won't post you back here under any circumstances and I want you here," and so I carried on happily for another year as Sergeant Bill.

The Armistice seemed to come upon us almost unnoticed, I think, because we were so busy but it happened and in "orders" issued to every Flying Station we read that "Hostilities will cease at 11:00 on November 11, 1918." As the hour approached, every driver stood by his or her vehicle and at a given signal blew their horns. The noise was deafening, the deep bass of the lorries' bulb horns, the tenor sounds from the Crossleys, and the high tones of the Fords. We were all brought to earth abruptly by a message: "All drivers report to the Detailing Office immediately." It appeared that arrangements had been made for a certain percentage of men and women on the station to be given leave and special trains were to be run from neighbouring stations. Needless to say, Transport Drivers could not be among the lucky ones for every vehicle would be needed to convey the troops to the stations. First the big lorries went off packed with cheering men and women and then the Crossleys set out for Pewsey. As the road from Central Flying School was all downhill or level, trailers were hitched on to accommodate a few more people. I know we were a very tired bunch of drivers who gathered in the Officers' Mess that evening to celebrate the end of the "War to end all Wars."

For the last seven months we had been nominally under the command of the WRAF officer, but I cannot remember that it made much difference. Saturday dances had gone on as usual and occasionally I was consulted by the C.O. as to a suitable punishment for some minor crime committed by a WRAF. Just before Christmas some United States Air Force officers had been posted to Central Flying School and most of us had got to know the flying officers fairly well, chiefly, I think, as a result of their inability to read a map. They were always having forced landings in the most out-of-the-way spots, miles off their prescribed course, and having come down they had great difficulty in giving their exact position. A party of Americans attending a celebration in the Officers' Mess was due to leave for home at 2230 hours by special train from Pewsey Station, and a few of our own officers who did not have their own cars as well as some of the M.T. girls decided to make an unauthorized trip in order to bid the Yanks farewell. Every girl answered to her name at 2200 hours roll call and then we slipped out, boarded a car, and made the run to the station. We should have realized that the C.O. and Senior officers would be on the platform. Obviously we were seen and recognized, but nothing was said until the next morning when the WRAF officer heard a rumour that Transport girls had broken out of camp. She went to the C.O. who knew that if we were put on a charge he would have to do the same to his own officers. I was asked if all my girls were in at roll call. How the old man soothed the troubled WRAF lady officer I do not know, but we heard no more of our late night jaunt.

When I first took over and signed for my Crossley Tender AM 6001 I thought it was, without doubt, the best car on Transport, and I certainly had no reason to ever change my opinion. On the steering wheel was carved, very neatly, the name J. Jordan and a regimental number, and I used to think a lot about Jordan and wondered if he was getting on all right in France and hoped that he would come through safely. By the end of 1919 most of the Transport were men and only about half a dozen M.T. girls remained to be demobilized. One day, a tall, middle-aged man appeared on the yard and made a beeline for 6001. It was J. Jordan, and he admitted that during his two and a half years in France he had often thought about his old car and hoped it had a good driver. He carved my name and number alongside his own and if anything could soften the blow of parting with 6001 it was the knowledge that J. Jordan was once more at the wheel.

During the whole of the year 1919 the great problem was how to keep the troops occupied. Matches were played between all the stations in our area and Transport was busy taking the rugger, soccer, hockey, tennis, and boxing teams to their various assignments. I had some very enjoyable trips with the Area Commanding Officer and Central Flying Commandant. They were both bachelors and were invited to all the big houses in the neighbourhood. I went to Longleat, Badminton, and Wilton for dances or shooting parties and was always made welcome at the Housekeepers' room. At last my demobilization papers came through and together with two other girls I started to pack up my belongings and to hand over 6001 and all my tools and other things in my charge. At the last minute it was discovered that I had signed for an American Bowser Petrol Pump and this piece of equipment had to be handed over to a Sergeant five minutes before I left the station. During 1920 I made a bit of money teaching ladies to drive and advising them with regard to the purchase of cars, and this phase lasted until my marriage in 1920.

CHAPTER VII:

Between the Wars
1920–1939

For a few years following her marriage in 1920, Nesta and her husband farmed in Sussex, a precarious occupation in those post-war days. They moved to North London in the mid-1920s where Norman got a job with a national dairy company.

Nesta's growing family kept her busy. She remained out of active Guiding until late 1932 when she was persuaded to take on a Ranger Company, girls sixteen or over. Press cuttings show that her Rangers took an active part in district events and performed many good turns for the needy people in the community. Nesta's love of camping had not diminished and she was able to arrange what must have been a somewhat unique camping experience for her girls.

During the few years of peace that remained before the outbreak of the Second World War, Nesta served as Captain of a Guide Company and as District Captain. She was a leading force in the acquisition by the district of its own Girl Guide District Headquarters. Nesta wrote very little about these years, which perhaps lacked some of the glamour of the pre-war pioneering days.

My demobilization did not come through until the end of 1919 and for the next twelve years Guiding, in my case, was confined to membership of the Local Association and a Trusteeship of the beautiful Guide Hall that was erected in my hometown of Crowborough. Marriage and the cares of family precluded any active participation in the Movement until 1932, by which time I was living in Hertfordshire. I was asked to take over a Ranger Company but soon found that the Company had been run on exactly the same lines that one would employ with girls of twelve years old, and although there were over twenty names on the roll, the average attendance was only four or five. Some of the girls were daughters of South Wales miners who had entered domestic service and many were definitely being exploited by their employers. Some mistresses I found cooperative and helpful, but in one or two cases I found the girl's only free time was a couple of hours off on a Sunday. Other girls were still at school and suffering from severe attacks of "Boyitis."

Obviously the only thing was to reorganize the programme entirely and I decided to have only fully qualified instructors in such things as First Aid, nursing, dressmaking, handicrafts, and nature. Once a month we had a talk by someone doing a special job: the buyer for one of the big London stores whose work took her to Paris every two weeks, a policewoman, the warden of an East End settlement, and many others. Boy friends were welcomed at these evenings, particularly towards Christmas when we started making and renovating toys. We also arranged many evening visits to such places as the General Post Office, a telephone exchange, a bakery, a milk bottling plant, and, most popular of all, a trip to the offices of the *London Times*. As all these London trips necessitated transport, we were helped enormously by an ex-Metropolitan police sergeant who ran a taxi business. He would take five girls at a time and deliver each one to her own house on return, charging only the cost of the gas. The girls, I know, enjoyed these trips and fully appreciated the fact that they were trusted to go on their own without the presence of a Guider.

As so many of the girls spent their working hours cooking and washing dishes, I felt that camping in the real sense would not be a holiday such as I wished for the girls to have. I was lucky enough to find a farm in Essex that took in guests. Here we pitched our tents in a field and had our camp fires which were well attended by the other guests and neighbouring farmers and their families. We cooked our own breakfast but our packed lunches and our big evening meals were supplied by the house. One morning the farmer came to us with the news that some cows had broken out of a meadow and asked if we could range the countryside in search of them. One or two girls went off on horseback and the rest scattered far and wide. Luckily I remained behind to help with the farm chores, for two hours later who should appear but the County Camp Advisor. What a sight met her eyes: half eaten breakfasts, dirty pots, tent brailing still down, beds unmade, a perfect example of bad camping! While I was trying to explain matters, two cows appeared driven by some of the dirtiest and most dishevelled Rangers one could imagine. The fact that the County Camp Advisor did not find it necessary to pay us a second visit and that my camp license was not withdrawn I always felt was quite a compliment.

When the district had to be divided it was suggested that I should become District Captain in the new area. This post I was quite willing to undertake until I found it really meant taking over the worst company in the county. "Quite unmanageable, hopeless, got rid of three Captains in a year, locked one Guider up in a cupboard under the stairs" — these were some of the things I was told about my new command. The first evening I found the girls were meeting in a little room barely large enough for one patrol so we had to make arrangements for the use of a big hall. We opened our meetings with the noisiest activity games I could think of which worked off some of the superfluous energy. Fortunately, they took to drill, military style, like ducks to water and in our first year we won a County Drill Competition. A few years later I met one of the ringleaders of the bad old days transformed into the smartest of A.T.S. Sergeants, and from her I had some heart-warming news of other girls who were doing well in the Armed Services. After the Second World War, I was frequently introduced to "my eldest girl in the Brownies"!

I was asked by a Ranger Captain to stage an emergency for a few girls who were having supper with her. So well did we perform that one of the Rangers actually turned faint. We arrived (my ten-year old-daughter and myself) outside the house with a fearsome crash (tin plates and a canister of stones) and much screaming. Out ran the Rangers to find a hysterical French woman with a broken wrist and a semi-conscious child with blood all over her face. When things had been cleared up successfully the girls realized that they had been tested — not only in the interpreter's job and first aid, but in their knowledge of the district. There had been phone calls to a doctor, ambulance service, police, a garage, and a bus depot asking them to deliver a message to the lady's brother who was meeting her there. On another occasion, I announced to my Guides that I should not be present at the beginning of the meeting, but would try and reach our hut later on unless they could recognize and challenge me by saying, "Excuse me, but are you Mrs. Jones?" I left my home as a rather bent old lady with a string bag and walking stick and managed to get on a bus under the very nose of one Guide. I finally got to within two hundred yards of my goal, but that time as a younger lady in a light coat and heavily made up, when up from a ditch popped a rather untidy Guide and Mrs. Jones was caught!

CHAPTER VIII:

The Second World War
1939–1945

The same week that war was declared Nesta and her two daughters were evacuated to a farm in Hampshire where they stayed for five months. As London had not been bombed as expected, there was a growing movement of evacuees back to their homes. Nesta's elder daughter joined the Land Army and later the WAAF, while her younger daughter was sent to boarding school. Nesta returned to her beloved London and to war service which, once again, saw her behind the wheel.

I spent the first five months of the Second World War in much the same way as I began the First—on a farm. I went to help as a milker on a big dairy farm in Hampshire. On my return to London I applied for membership in the Women's Voluntary Service, a recognized arm of Civil Defence under the Home Office. The interview seemed to be going badly. I expressed my willingness to do anything, but "No, I was a very poor needlewoman and could not cut out garments or use a sewing machine." I had to admit to being a fairly good plain cook but with no experience of cooking for large numbers and "No, I couldn't use a typewriter or a switchboard." Of course, I could milk cows, raise vegetables, make jam and drive anything, but the WVS seemed to have no use for these skills until the interviewer asked, "Have you ever driven with a trailer?" Then I could truthfully say yes, and I was introduced to "Mexico." The ladies of the British colony in Mexico had presented the WVS with a mobile canteen and Morris car with which to tow it. Throughout the London Blitz "Mexico" served food in every big "incident" (as the destruction caused by a bomb was called) and many small incidents in every part of the metropolitan area and beyond. The grey canteen had painted on one side the words "Presented to the Women's Voluntary Services by the Ladies of the English Colony of Mexico." This inscription no doubt was the reason for a policeman bringing up one of his colleagues and saying, "Now you'll be OK, mate. The Mexico women are wonderful!" As I spent so much time in this canteen it might be as well if I tried to describe its interior. Entering at the back on the immediate left were the racks of mugs from floor to ceiling, next to a clear counter space in front of the serving hatch with room for a ten-gallon Thermos tea urn and a rack of mugs. Facing the entrance were two Primus stoves and an oil stove on which could be fitted a small oven in which we heated meat pies or sausage rolls. The Primus stoves were used for boiling water for the endless cups of tea. On the right hand side opposite the mug rack was the sink and another expanse of counter on which sandwiches were cut or buns buttered. Above and below this counter were cupboards filled with cans of soup and milk, babies' bottles, coffee, cocoa, cigarettes, chewing gum, sugar, and anything we could think of that might conceivably be asked for at 2:00 a.m. in the middle of an air raid.

'Mexico', Sept 1940

As the name implies, the WVS was very largely a voluntary organization. Apart from a small administrative staff in London, nearly all
the centres were run by women who gave their services freely and
willingly in whichever branch they felt they could be most useful. The
green and maroon uniform, whether it was overall, dress, or suit,
became nearly as well known as that of the Services. In addition to
driving the canteen, I also used my own car on behalf of the WVS
and the first job I had was to help with evacuees from West Ham.
They arrived in East Barnet by bus and after a meal at one of the
church halls, catered for by the Rest Centre personnel of the WVS,
they were allotted their billets and taken there by voluntary car
drivers. I noticed a little old couple sitting rather apart from the rest
and not eating so I approached them and was at once seized by
the wife. Her husband, it seemed, was a diabetic and had missed

his insulin that day. I hurried to the Medical Officer on duty and we picked out a most suitable billet where the hostess was a trained nurse and her father just the right age to be companionable to the old couple. It happened that I had my lovely black poodle with me and as we had to call the chemist to get the insulin, I thought it better to leave him behind knowing he would do his duty by amusing the children. When I got back I found Robin surrounded by children and cheerfully obeying every command to sit or shake a paw and catching bits of bun thrown at him. One of the borough officials advised me to give him a soft cushion to sit on when we got home!

Although there was plenty of work for the canteen and its crew in the summer of 1940, it was not until December that its first big test came. The duties of the four women who made up the crew of "Mexico" were as follows: driver, relief driver, leader, and mate. I was very lucky in my relief driver, Audrey. She and I between us could, I believe, turn the outfit on a sixpence. I had perfect confidence that Audrey would give me every inch and she knew that the moment she raised her hand the car would stop. Many times during an awkward manoeuvre, a man would suggest he should take the wheel or he would try to give me directions until told firmly to "Shut up!" Then he would either retire grumbling about women drivers or wait to see the end of the performance when he would say, "I never thought you'd make it, good work!" In December 1940, the phone by my bed rang at 4:00 a.m. and the Centre Organizer's voice said, "Would you go to Bristol with the canteen, leaving at once?" Service in the Royal Flying Corps had taught me the wisdom of always keeping an overnight bag ready packed, so in ten minutes I was away. The first duty of the driver was to rouse the local baker who always had twelve loaves ready for us. Next call was at the dairy to pick up a crate of milk, and then back to hitching up the canteen. Meantime the other three members of the team had got an urn of tea ready and all the necessary makings for sandwiches: butter, corned beef, salmon, and potted meat. Because this was our first overnight assignment, we decided to take one blanket and pillow each feeling that if we were stranded we could drive a mile or two out of the city and sleep, two in the canteen and two in the car. The Civil Defence Transport Officer came over with directions as to the route, but I knew the Great West Road quite well and decided to take the first shift while it was dark.

At 5:00 a.m. we were ready to leave and we soon left London behind us. Approaching Newbury, I handed over to Audrey and retired to the back seat for a sleep after telling her the route— Newbury, Hungerford, Marlborough, and Bath, practically a direct road. I woke up to find that we were taking corners and bends which certainly were not on the Great West Road and poor Audrey confessed she had been diverted just east of Newbury and had never been brought back to the Great West Road again. As we appeared to be heading for Whitchurch and Basingstoke, I decided to take a shortcut via Ludgershall, Upavon, and Devizes to Bath on the principle that a road one knows is usually quicker than an unknown way. Our first stop occurred about four miles short of my old station, the Central Flying School. An army patrol told us the road through CFS was closed and we would certainly be turned back. In spite of this, I decided to risk it. Sure enough we were halted, but by the time I had shown our credentials and explained the urgency of the trip and demanded firmly to see the Orderly Officer or the Adjutant, the Sergeant rather unwillingly let us through with a chit for his opposite number at the other end of the closure. After that we made fast time to Devizes where we were stopped by a motorcyclist policeman who said he would have to summons me for pulling a trailer without having an outside mirror on the car. After apologizing and accepting the summons we explained our mission and were told the main road into Bath had been bombed out but our policeman said he would lead us round another way and we were very soon running into Bath. I realized now that on arrival at Bristol we should have to fill up with petrol immediately, and if the town had been badly blitzed this might not be easy. We pulled up at a fire station on the outskirts of Bath and asked if they could fill our tank. At first we met with a very firm refusal. We must go to the City Hall and obtain a chit from the Civil Defence and take this to some other office to be countersigned and then come back having wasted probably an hour. Never have I worked so hard, but after ten minutes of my pleading, cajoling, and chaffing, the boss man relented and not only filled our tank but sent a car to lead us right into Bristol where we arrived soon after 11:00 a.m., just over 120 miles in six hours.

It seemed to me that we had hardly stopped outside Bristol Town Hall and our leader, Doris, was barely out of the car when a young fellow put his head through the window and said, "I'm your guide and I know where we've got to go." Twenty minutes later we were serving tea, cutting sandwiches, and I was pumping up my Primus stoves and exchanging cockney backchat with the London Fire Brigade men who had been sent for before midnight. It was not long before the food we had brought with us was finished and we were sent to a workhouse where WVS volunteers were cutting sandwiches and filling tea urns as fast as it was possible to do so. We were so busy I, for one, had not given a thought to accommodation for the night but a message reached us to say we were billeted with the Regional Commissioner, Sir Hugh Elles. As soon as a relief canteen arrived I dropped the other three at the house and went on to a garage round the corner where I left the car to be thoroughly checked and filled up. Sir Hugh, well known to World War One veterans as the commander of the earliest tanks, was a charming host, and as we dined well and went to bed early we woke next morning rested and ready for what the day might bring.

We were so busy and it was so cold I really have little recollection of what we did. The cold was so intense that the water from the fire hoses froze and the tea we served had ice on it before it reached the men. We were very saddened to hear of the tragic death of the driver of the Bristol Canteen who was drowned when her car went over the dock side in the dark. The third day we were recalled and started for London in convoy with the London Fire Brigade. As it was still cold, we were only too glad to accept their invitation to stop in Marlborough for a warm up! I stuck to beer, which affected me less than gin and ginger, the tipple chosen by the rest of the team!

Another incident "Mexico" was involved in occurred on April 16, 1941, the worst raid on London. We had been out early in the evening to a small local incident which was closed as we got there. There was obviously trouble building up in London, and as the canteen was fully stocked and ready to move at a minute's notice we decided to spend the night on the floor of the office. It so happened that a bale of blankets had been delivered that day so we were comfortable and after notifying the authorities we settled down to a good night. Not for long though. At about 2:30 a.m. the phone rang with the order to report to Westminster Civil Defence Centre. Just past Lord's Cricket Ground the road was closed so I turned into Regent's Park and came out into Portland Place. The British Broadcasting Corporation had been badly hit and as we picked our way through the rubble we were shouted at and begged to stop. Knowing that Westminster would probably not expect us for half an hour we spent ten minutes serving the tired Rescue and Fire Brigade men. Then we went on to the Westminster Underground Headquarters and, as I was acting leader, I ran in to report "East Barnet Canteen reporting for duty." I explained we had stopped in Portland Place and it appeared that it had been the officer's intention to send us there first. The staff were amazed at the speed with which we had answered their call and we were called Flying Angels, Lightning Ladies, and so on. Instructions were to go to an alley behind the Hippodrome called Little Newport Place which leads into Gerrard Street, but when I saw how narrow the alley was I sent Mrs. Swift, my second-in-command, to find the Incident Officer and ask if we might enter Gerrard Street from Shaftesbury Avenue. It so happened that on that particular night I was operating without one of our regular team. Mrs. Swift, a World War One veteran, was tremendous, quietly getting on with the job and directing the two young girls, neither of whom had ever worked in the canteen before. One, in fact, was not even a member of the WVS. Mrs. Swift came back having found out exactly where the Incident Officer wanted the canteen stationed and with orders to feed everybody. She said the street was packed with excitable, hysterical foreigners, most of whom appeared to have forgotten what English they ever knew. In fact, a typical Soho crowd! As we pulled up in Gerrard Street, the crowd surged towards us and for a moment I actually feared for the safety of the canteen. Leaving the girls to get everything set up inside but with orders not to open the serving hatch until told, Mrs. Swift and I fought our way into the crowd and gradually by means of signs and my limited French and Mrs. Swift's fairly fluent Italian we got a long, but co-operative queue in order, opened the hatch and the rush was on!

Obviously our food was not going to last any time and I had to replenish the stocks. Nearly opposite to us was a baker's shop, the floor covered with loaves so I quickly found a policeman and with the authority of the law I collected enough bread to last for hours and locked it in the car. Then the policeman found a grocer's shop knee-deep in tins and containers and at the back of the shop we discovered a big zinc bath. We were just filling this with tins of salmon, butter, milk, corned beef, tongue, biscuits, and so on when the owner appeared. Our orders were never to go "looting" without authority and to try and keep some account of what we took. On this occasion the proprietor, a Welshman, urged us to take everything.

He was so thankful that he and his wife had escaped uninjured that he wanted to show his gratitude by helping the less fortunate. Seeing he was no longer needed, my policeman went back to help the Incident Officer and later on he beckoned me across and told me that Winston Churchill and Mr. Morrison, the Home Secretary, had visited the canteen while I was away, and had stood by the door and asked Mrs. Swift when the canteen had arrived. Without really looking up she had replied, "About three o'clock I think, but if you want serving you will have to go to the back of the queue. I haven't got time to talk!" Later on someone told her who the visitors were but Mrs. Swift's only reaction was, "I don't care who they were, I still didn't have time to talk!"

Among the people in the crowd we noticed several service men, mostly youngsters who had been bombed out of a hostel and were helping the Rescue men. One young sailor in particular stood out. He wandered about obviously dazed and shocked. I tried to persuade him to come and sit on the canteen steps and have a cup of tea, but he would only shake his head and resume his aimless drifting. A Red Cross Ambulance was drawn up near us and I pointed the lad out to the doctor who said she had failed to get through to him at all. I had by then located my water supply in the basement of a school. The taps were still running from the tank in the attic. Unfortunately, I was not able to get my bucket under the taps because of the little children's sized washbasins underneath. I borrowed a heavy hammer from a Rescue crew and approached my sailor and told him I wanted a man's help. At first he hung back but by degrees I edged him away from the crowd and into the basement. Without speaking I showed him the problem and handed him the hammer. The destruction that boy wrought in two minutes on three basins was terrific and after we had filled the buckets I took off my jacket and tie and had a good wash, and then I told the lad I had always wanted to see what a sailor wore under his jumper.

Slowly he stripped and took the face cloth and towel I threw to him. When we were clean we beat the dust out of our uniforms, combed our hair, picked up our buckets, and returned to the canteen. All this time the boy had not spoken but the dazed look was gone. After he had had a good meal of soup and sandwiches, I suggested he go out on the next ambulance for a check up, thinking perhaps the shock had left him dumb but the answer came loud and clear, "Hell no, I'm going to help those fellows dig," and off he went.

Near to us a girl had been located, alive but trapped and the doctor was anxious to get some refreshment down to her but the opening into her prison was only a tiny hole. We at once produced a milk bottle full of tea and a long rubber tube that could be inserted into the hole and through which nourishment could be taken. When the girl was finally brought to the surface I think tears were mixed with sweat on the Rescue men's faces.

At about 11:00 a.m. Mrs. Swift and I decided to find some refreshment other than canteen food and, leaving the two girls in charge, we walked across Piccadilly Circus to the Criterion Restaurant. We found a long queue and were told they were serving smoked salmon sandwiches and beer as water, gas, and electricity services were all disrupted. Luckily for us, the maitre d'hotel had seen the canteen arrive and we were brought forward and asked to explain who we were. In the dining room two Army officers had just finished their meal and were requested to leave, which they did at once giving us their table. I think even now, after nearly thirty-five years, that meal was the best I have ever eaten. The bill certainly was a shock but it was handed to us stamped "Paid." We were assured that our two helpers would receive the same courtesy.

By four o'clock no relief had arrived from our centre and I walked back to Westminster Civil Defense Centre and phoned. We had been completely forgotten, but I was promised that four ladies would be with us in half an hour. Unfortunately, when they arrived not one had been on the canteen before and no one was capable of driving the trailer back. In any case, the owner of the car that brought them would not allow any one else to drive her car. This meant that we had to unhitch Mexico and leave it while I drove my exhausted team home in the Morris. Later in the evening Audrey and I went down and she brought the canteen home.

On two occasions the canteen was called out at midnight to serve men working on projects but what the projects were we only discovered weeks later. The first call was to Enfield, a small town only five miles from home, but as we drove through to the Town Hall we could not see any damage. We picked up a police escort and were then led right out into the country, and finally halted in the middle of a field and told to get ready for customers in ten minutes. When the customers arrived they proved to be members of an Irish Pioneer Corps, some Heavy Rescue men, and a few surveyors with instruments and maps but all, without exception, were plastered with mud and obviously tired and hungry. When the first shift had been fed and rested and a few minor injuries patched up, the men returned to work, but what that work was, we had no idea. All night the gangs alternated and I had to keep a bucket of warm water handy for the men to rinse their hands in before they could touch a sandwich and when we left at 6:00 a.m. we were no wiser as to what they were doing. The truth was that one of the main water conduits into London had been cut by a bomb and a large part of the Capital was threatened with no water. Reference to a map showed that there was an old wooden conduit leading from the new River Reservoir, which, if it could be located and cleared, could serve as a temporary outlet to London. On another occasion we were called to the London Docks and again we served a variety of customers from skilled craftsmen to Irish navvies. It was not until after D-Day that we learned that all those men had been employed on building PLUTO (Pipe-Line Under The Ocean) and the prefabricated harbour called Mulberry, without which the invasion of France would not have been possible.

May 10, 1941, was the worst raid on London after April 16, and we were called to Whitechapel and stationed near Fenchurch Street in the heart of the blazing city. We were welcomed on the site by some of the firemen we had met in Bristol, one of whom yelled, "OK boys, here's Mexico!" They then explained that they had hoses and booster pumps laid to the river but needed some water with which to prime the pumps to start them working. It was our proud boast that we were never asked for anything we were unable to supply and water was soon forthcoming. About 4:00 a.m. an agitated warden told us to move off at once as an unexploded bomb had buried itself quite near the canteen and the Bomb Disposal Unit would probably not arrive in time. We hastily secured everything loose in the canteen, jumped into the car, and drove off. My idea, of course, was to put as many buildings between me and the bomb as possible so we kept turning corners and finally pulled up completely lost. A policeman gave us detailed directions on how to reach home but no sooner had we left him than I asked the other members of the team what he had said. They all admitted they had not even listened, thinking that I, as driver, would take it all in. We asked again for directions and this time four people listened intently to what was said, but a mile further on we were again lost and we realized the truth, we were too tired to take in anything! From then on I just drove quietly until it became light enough to recognize a known landmark. I was not surprised when our Transport Officer rang up to know if we had enjoyed our trip to the sea! We had taken forty miles to do what should have been a fifteen-mile journey.

The night that St. Paul's Cathedral was threatened we stood in a lane a few hundred yards away. The hard pavement was cracked and the fireman's hoses had washed up the London clay into a sea of gluey mud. I happened that night to be wearing rubber soled shoes and when I started to drive home my feet slipped off the pedals and I had to take off both shoes and stockings in order to drive safely.

Many little human dramas were played out in the privacy of the Mexico Canteen. A man whose wife had been dug out and taken to hospital and whose baby son was missing asked if he could come inside and pull himself together. A few minutes later a fireman arrived carrying a screaming baby "Cradle had caught on rafter back at the 'ouse," he explained. "Had to get our long ladder. Don't think the nipper's hurt!" Five minutes later Dad was feeding his hungry son from a bottle of warm milk and water. A week or two later a letter was received at the WVS Headquarters in London addressed to "The Ladies on Mexico Canteen." It said, "Wife and baby doing fine and thanks for all you did at the Welsh Harp raid." This was only one of many such letters.

As the war progressed, Queen's Messenger Convoys were stationed at strategic points all over England. These Convoys were made up of two water tanks weighing six tons loaded, a stores lorry, a kitchen van, five canteens, and a station wagon, and in addition each convoy had a motorcycle dispatch rider who acted as sheepdog and kept the vehicles moving. If a convoy had to go through a large town the dispatch rider would phone ahead and it would be met by a police escort. The Queen's Messenger Convoys could prepare hot stew and dessert for hundreds of people, and in addition to the WVS ladies those in the front line had the invaluable help of some strong young men who were members of the Friends Society. These lads did all the heavy lifting of the boilers and sacks of flour, sugar, potatoes, and so on. We all admired them and even our dispatch rider, who was very against conscientious objectors, admitted that they more than pulled their weight in Civil Defence, even if their consciences would not permit them to carry arms.

Queen's Messengers Convoy, Nesta second from left

The first call we had was to Mitcham and we were short of a canteen driver. Although I usually drove one of the water carts, Smith, our dispatch rider, called to me to get on one of the Bedford 30 cwt. canteens. As I had never driven one of these vehicles it took me a few moments to locate the self-starter, but having found it I made haste to catch up with the van ahead. Meanwhile, Smith was riding alongside and shouting at me to "put my ruddy lights on." I tried every switch and failed to find the right one and Smithy's language got more and more lurid! At last they went on! Arriving at Mitcham, I climbed out of my seat to be met by Smithy who greeted me with apologies. "Oh Bill," he said, "I thought you were one of them ruddy Conchies."

When South London, Croydon, and Tooting seemed to be the target, we were stationed on Beckenham Golf Links, nearly an hour's run from East Barnet, and as we had to be on duty by 7:00 a.m. it meant an early start. The ten vehicles were dispersed over the fairways at night and my first job every morning was to walk out and bring in the vans in the order in which they would be needed: first the kitchen with its six boilers and fuel, then the water tank and stores, and lastly the canteens. One morning one of the cars would not start so I left it and walked on to the next one. Just then the engine of a passing doodlebug cut out, a sure sign it was coming down, so I dived under the nearest van in time to see the non-starter go up in a thousand bits. Naturally, the rest of the twenty-member team thought I was one of the bits and I got a wonderful welcome!

Most of us were sorry to leave our old Mexico Mobile Canteen. The Queen's Messengers operated only in the daytime and served mostly civilians still able to live in their damaged houses but who had been deprived of all cooking facilities. No doubt we did good work, but the convoys were organized by the Ministry of Food and we felt we were just Civil Servants with little freedom of action. We missed the thrill and excitement of the fast drives to incidents and the close liaison with the Heavy and Light Rescue men, the police and firemen. We were under orders and frequently became entangled in red tape. I remember once, going to a street and finding that no hot meals had been delivered for over thirty-six hours. As we had been sent out only with tea and sandwiches for men working on repairs we could do little to placate the irate and hungry housewives. Luckily, Smithy arrived at that moment and we sent him back to base to ask for hot stew for two hundred people. Meanwhile, we told the crowd that we would be back in half an hour and that they were to collect any receptacles they could find and when they heard the motor horn they were to come out and line up and everyone would be fed. It so happened that some high officials from the Ministry of Food were visiting our base that day and Smithy said they obviously did not believe that two hundred people in one street had not been fed and stew for fifty would be sent and that would be enough. We gathered later that Smith and our WVS organizer had united in saying firmly that if Ashworth wanted stew for two hundred she was going to get stew for two hundred, and no less! The Ministry of Food officials, only half convinced, followed us back in their car in time to witness the line up of women with their basins, buckets, dish pans, and in one case a lovely chamber pot with pink roses on it—"Only thing left big enough for six of us, mate!"

One never knew what the next request would be. I have seen six policemen sitting in the road overcome by escaping gas being bullied by an elderly WVS lady to drink strong black coffee. Then she almost dragged them to their feet and kept them walking till medical help arrived. One of the rescue dogs was given into our charge one night. He had been injured by a falling beam while carrying out his duty of locating buried persons. We made him a bed on our overcoats and fed him warm milk and brandy and I am glad to say he made a good recovery. For a few nights I drove a canteen for Greenwich and my mate on those occasions was a seventeen-year-old girl waiting to join the WRNS. After a particularly unpleasant night we were going home in a tram and had to listen to a long tirade by a typical "Colonel Blimp" who informed everybody that the raids would be over in a week or two. He had seen fifteen doodlebugs shot down at the mouth of the Thames that night! My little friend leaned forward, touched him on the knee and said, "All I can say, Sir, is there were a heck of a lot you didn't see brought down!"

At the end of the War many of the Queen's Messenger convoys

were presented to European countries to help with their rehabilitation. East Barnet WVS centre, which had consistently used women drivers on all its vehicles throughout the war, was given the honour of driving all the five London-based Convoys to their embarkation ports. We took two to Liverpool, one to Cardiff, one to Bristol, and one to London docks.

After VE day life seemed to be a succession of farewell parties and parades. Although Barnet is actually in the County of Hertfordshire we were so close to the County of London boundary that we were included in the London Region for Civil Defence. This meant that, in addition to our own County rallies, we were invited to take part in the Farewell March Past and Inspection by King George VI and Queen Elizabeth. This was in May 1945, and I and Mrs. Godfrey were detailed to take a huge mobile kitchen to Hyde Park to supply boiling water to about one hundred small mobile canteens waiting to refresh the weary marchers after their long trek round the Outer Circle. On our way to the Park we passed a barrow boy selling cherries. It was a very hot day but we doubted if it was worth stopping as the queue was so long. However, Godfrey jumped out and was soon back with a whole pound of cherries and tears streaming down her cheeks. She said the crowd had literally swallowed her up, insisted on her going to the front of the line, and had quite overwhelmed her with their gratitude "for what you ladies did for my old man, our kids," and so on.

Knowing that once the march past began we would be busy, I snatched a few minutes before it started and strolled down to where the rescue dogs were stationed. I knew the handler for he had been in charge of the dog who had been injured in an incident and brought to the canteen. While we were chatting, the Queen and Princess Elizabeth arrived and were told of the dog's injury and I was introduced. Soon four people were talking about dogs like old friends.

CHAPTER IX:

From England to Canada
1945–1982

After the war, Nesta renewed her long association with the Girl Guides. Camping had always been one of her major interests, but now it was camping with a difference—camping with physically handicapped Guides.

In 1951, Nesta suffered the first of a number of heart attacks, but she learned to live with her "wonky heart" as she called it, and after spending a year in Vancouver with her two daughters she decided to make it her home for the last thirty years of her life.

By 1946 I had decided that having been out of active Guiding for so many years the time had come to really hang up my boots and gracefully retire, and I firmly refused all offers of Companies, Commissionerships, and even clerical jobs. I remained Badge Secretary and almost without knowing how it happened I found myself adopted into Extensions as a driver and as a pusher of wheelchairs. The Extension Branch of Guiding started in a very big orthopaedic hospital in Southern England. Some of the girls got hold of *Scouting for Boys* and started tapping out the Morse code on their cups, signalling, and throwing life lines from one bed to another. Luckily, some of the nurses co-operated, and the doctors and staff soon realized that the game of Guiding and the feeling of belonging to a vast sisterhood was having a very good effect on many of their patients. But what would happen to the girls when they went home? Many of them couldn't be active Guides. So Post Guides (later called Extensions) was started, run on the same lines as Lone Guides but geared to handicapped girls.

No one who has not actually been in close contact with severely handicapped girls can have any idea of what it means to feel oneself an active member of a worldwide movement. But small things, too, can mean so much to a girl whose life from childhood has been bounded by a hospital, an institution, or the four walls of her own home. At the first Extension camp I attended every girl was asked if there was anything special she would like to do. Such humble requests were made. An epileptic wanted to have her hair shampooed, waved, and set at a "real" hairdresser's; another's idea of bliss was tea in a very grand restaurant; others wanted to go in a boat, visit a theatre, see the local aquarium, and of course, go shopping. How good people are to crippled Guides! Stores that normally would not allow chairs to block up the gangways would go out of their way to make things easy, or would bring goods out into the street in order that the customer could make her own choice. The aquarium visit looked like being a problem as the only approach was down a long flight of steep stone steps which would necessitate four strong people to carry each chair. No sooner was the first party in position (I was on a front wheel) when four men appeared, cheerfully remarking, "Now, you just tell us what to do and we'll do it!" After the rounds had been made, there they were waiting with several recruits to get everyone up again, and believe me, it was no easy job!

Although I had been to two hostel camps with the same girls, I could hardly believe it when I was asked to be a "universal aunt" with the first party to go to Switzerland in June 1950. I think there were about fourteen handicapped girls and ten "Pushers," including an interpreter, a doctor, and a nurse. The professional duties of the last named proved to be very light and our only casualty was the doctor who fell down some steps and bruised her back! It is impossible here to describe all the thrills of that trip from the moment when we all met to collect passports and travellers' cheques to the return to the airport where the Customs officials smilingly waved aside our carefully prepared lists of purchases!

I was told that one of my duties was to be custodian of Jane. Well, I thought Jane was a poor little handicapped girl who perhaps needed special attention. But she wasn't. Jane was the bedpan! You cannot travel with handicapped girls on a long journey without a bedpan. But when Jane was handed to me she was in a state of complete nudity. So the first thing I did for Jane was to make her a nice, navy blue serge uniform, and I embroidered a trefoil in the middle of it and on either side I embroidered "B-P." When somebody asked me what it meant, I said, "Baden-Powell." I thought afterwards that possibly "Be Prepared" would have been a better answer!"

We arrived in Paris at 11:30 a.m. having flown from London and were taken to a hotel where accommodation had been booked by the French Guides who later entertained us to tea at their offices. Also visiting were two USA Girl Scouts and there was much comparison and discussion on the blue, brown, and green uniforms. After a restful night in Paris we boarded a train for Interlaken, and at the French frontier we were met by Swiss Guides who came to the station to call greetings and pass cookies through the windows of the train and then we all sang Guide songs. Normally, the party should have changed trains at Basle but the Swiss guard came along to say that our coach would be switched to a siding and joined on to the other train. "No trouble, no trouble at all, Madame," and that was Switzerland! Next day, some of us went into town to collect money and the bank clerks came out into the street to obtain the necessary signatures. People strolled up and chatted to the girls, not because they were cripples, but because they were Guides in uniform and recognized as such. The only discordant note I heard was from an Englishwoman when I was helping a spastic girl make a purchase. The child in question happened to possess an extremely appreciative and alert brain and heard the remark, "How stupid to bring those girls out here. They can't enjoy the scenery or anything." I am afraid that brought me to a battle with some good, sound, home truths!

In 1951 I was hospitalized for over two months which definitely ended my role as a Pusher, but I was still able to chauffeur Extensions to field days, rallies, and camps, and that same year I went to Wood Larks, the special Extension Camp situated in Surrey. One Sunday, just as visitors were leaving, one of the worst storms ever to hit that part of the country suddenly broke. Thunder roared, lightning flashed, and the rain came down in torrents. In an instant every able-bodied man and Guider rushed to bring in the wheelchairs, close the shutters of the open air shelter, and rescue the tents and bedding, and I could not even lift a mattress! This feeling of being useless lasted about two minutes until the first chair cases arrived with their occupants soaked through, scared and frightened by the severity of the storm. Dry clothes, warm blankets, hot drinks, cheerful talk were all within my powers to provide, and in no time at all it seemed we were all safely under cover drinking cocoa and singing Camp fire songs at the tops of our voices.

In the autumn of 1951 I sailed for Canada in company with my younger daughter on a visit to my elder girl who had settled in Vancouver. We wore our World badges and had many a pleasant chat with Guides and Guiders during the crossing, and the pin was recognized at once by our waiter on the long train journey across Canada. His wife was a Guider and had it not been for the nature of his employment he would have liked to be in Scouts. My daughter had started Brownies in Chinatown and I was intensely interested in the mixed nationalities of the Pack: Chinese, Japanese, Black, and White. The colour made no difference, all were Brownies.

Chinatown Brownies, Vancouver 1951

During my first year in Canada the Chief Guide visited British Columbia and as we had not actually met for some years I sent a short welcoming note to the local office and, to my surprise, received an invitation to a meeting at which she was speaking. This led to an invitation to take over the visiting of enrolled Guides and Brownies who might happen to be patients in the Children's Hospital as well as those who wanted to join, and for some years I became both Captain and Brown Owl to a succession of children of all ages. Many of the patients were long-term cases, lying in plaster casts for months and working their way steadily through Tenderfoot and Recruits' tests till the goal of Enrolment was reached. One three-bed ward in particular seemed to attract Brownies. There was Caroline who had never walked properly, and to whom we gave a special

Grand Howl to celebrate her first faltering steps; Gloria who spent months lying on her face but who passed all her tests with flying colours; Doreen, Barbara, Helen, and many more, most of whom continued in Guiding in their own localities after they left the hospital. Increasing deafness forced me to give up the visiting in 1959.

**Queen Alexandra Solarium, Christmas 1957
Guiders and Guides from 1st Brentwood
Company, Saanich Division, V.I.**

When I first arrived in British Columbia I was struck by the wonderful possibilities for camping and hiking. The open country, the woods, lakes, and rivers seemed to offer such glorious opportunities, but a conversation with a hospitalized Guide from up north soon opened my eyes to the fact that things are not always what they seem! "No," she said rather sadly, "we can't do much hiking. You see, we mustn't go beyond a certain area unless the cougar hunter can come with us!" I learned that in another area, it was impossible to pitch tents or sleep out because of bears, and yet another locality was barred on account of rattlesnakes! Soon after I arrived I was told by an elderly lady that she was going to camp that summer. Having myself reached the age when I was beginning to prefer my creature comforts to the joys of camp I was greatly impressed by this display of energy, until I learned that "camp" consisted of a six-room cottage with electricity laid on and all the "mod cons." This "misuse" of the word camp led me astray on several occasions. I even found that Guide camp frequently meant sleeping in four-bunk cabins, cooking on a stove, and eating in the recreation hut with china and cutlery supplied by the camp. Some of the older girls spoke of having been to Pioneer camps where they did sleep in tents and cook on campfires.

1960, being Jubilee year, brought me many pleasant invitations to various companies who showed intense interest in stories of the old days. During the celebrations many companies put on skits and sketches showing Guiding as they imagined it to have been in 1910. Sometimes I was consulted as to what girls did wear in those days. One Guide even rang up to know what coloured shorts I wore at the Crystal Palace! Sometimes, I am sorry to say, we were depicted as a lot of round-shouldered, sloppy children by girls who slouched onto the stage for the purpose only of raising a laugh from the audience. No doubt we looked funny to the present generation with our long skirts, big hats, water bottles, stretcher slings, and haversacks, but drill was such an important part of Guide training in those days that I am quite sure we could have given points to any present day Company for smartness in marching and appearance.

EPILOGUE

Although Nesta was forced to give up active Guiding, she continued to attend Guide events whenever she could.

In 1972, while on holiday in England, she visited Margaret Harris who had been Captain of the 1st Richmond Company in the early days and who had accompanied Nesta and the others on the camping trip to the Lake District in 1912. That same afternoon she met Lady Baden-Powell for the last time. The two elderly ladies sat together for more than an hour talking about old times, and then, arm-in-arm, walked slowly down the long corridor of Lady Baden-Powell's "Grace and Favour" apartment in Hampton Court to the door and parted. That night in her diary Nesta wrote, "Everyone getting old."

In 1973, she crossed Canada from Vancouver to Montreal by car driven by her elder daughter. In every town where they stopped she met with Guides and Guiders and told them the story of how Guides began. She spoke on radio and television and gave interviews to the press. On her return to British Columbia, Girl Guides honoured her with a life membership.

Although Nesta's heart gave cause for concern, she was able to make one final visit to England in June 1977. She returned to her old hometown of Crowborough where a party was arranged to welcome her back to the Guide Company she had started in 1912. She met not only present-day Guides but four of the original Guides, now grandmothers.

Many changes had taken place in Guiding from those early days to the present, and from time to time Nesta reflected on those changes.

Whenever old (or should one say, elderly) Guides get together the question is sure to be asked: has Guiding lost its adventure? I would reply that if it has, it is due to a lack of imagination on the part of both Captain and Guides.

Camping in the early days was a real adventure and one of my first experiences was as a very junior assistant to Miss Maynard at a camp near Sittingbourne in Kent. We were all housed in a huge barn and the officers were given hammocks to sleep in. Never shall I forget that first night! In one side and out the other seemed to be the pattern, and even after I had mastered the art of staying put the night seemed very long, and when Miss Maynard agreed to let us put up tents we were a very grateful band of juniors. Even tracking I think was made more interesting in the old days. We used to prepare patches of dirt and girls would walk or ride a bicycle across leaving tracks from which the other tried to guess the pace they used and whether they were carrying a weight or travelling light. Of course, many country companies possessed a pair of tracking irons, which left the mark of an animal's hoof.

Two facets of Guiding come to mind in which I believe the old timers excelled. The first was the practical application of the motto "Be prepared." So much early training began with the words "If you saw—if you were—or if such and such were to happen—what would you do?" I would often ask my Guides such questions as the following: "On the way to school, suppose you saw smoke coming out of Mrs. Smith's cottage window. Would you run back to the crossroads and look for help, or try to get into the cottage? You know Mrs. Smith is deaf, so if you had to break a window, how would you do it? With your fist, or would you remember to take off a shoe? If the smoke was thick have you a scarf or anything to tie round your mouth? Is there a puddle or a water butt you could soak it in?" And so on and so forth until the day came when a similar situation did occur, and it happened to one of my own Guides. She reacted splendidly and was heartily congratulated by everyone concerned. How to deal with a runaway horse or a savage dog were routine questions in those days and we all knew what to do if we found anything of value from a lost child to money.

The second thing we took so seriously was the Good Turn, which in the early days was a purely individual effort. The collective or Company Good Turn did not come into being until much later. At first we followed strictly the Chief Scout's suggestion to tie the ends of our scarves in a knot until we had done our Good Turn for the day. Some Captains made their Guides recite aloud before the company the kind actions they had carried out during the past week. The Forest Mere Company never did that, but we did suggest once or twice that we should all write down without giving names some of the good things we had done without being either asked or told to do. I remember well some of these Good Turns. The smallest Sunflower in my patrol had spent the whole of one Saturday morning at the bottom of a steep hill clutching a small log of wood. If a vehicle approached with the horse wearing a bearing rein, the child would politely request the driver to open it. If the cart was loaded she would trudge behind ready to "scotch" a wheel with her billet so as to give the horse a rest. One of the Scarlet Pimpernels had gone to school armed with oil and a feather because the iron gate squeaked so. As every mother knows, shopping with small children can be quite a chore, but housewives in one village knew that after three o'clock when school was out there would be one or two of "those Scout girls" willing to amuse the toddlers while mother bought the groceries. It always seemed easier to find personal Good Turns to do in the country than in a town which was, I think, the reason we used to stress to town Guides the importance of obedience to teachers, the ready smile and kind word for the stranger, keeping the roads clear of litter, giving way to older people in a bus, and offering to carry heavy bags.

(The following are closing remarks from a talk given at the Girl Guides Annual Meeting in British Columbia in 1968)

I don't believe there is a Guider here who hasn't had the experience of the meeting that went wrong—the game that was to have been such tremendous fun but that went over like a pricked balloon, and in patrol time all they did was to natter about their boyfriends, and when you practised the horseshoe they slopped round with their heads poked forward, flatfooted, looking like refugees from the chain gang. All you wanted to do was see the back of the kids, turn out the light, get home, and write your resignation! We've all had those evenings. But have you had this experience? When you got to the door, you found a girl looking at the toes of her shoes mumbling something about, "Can I speak to you, Captain?" You had to forget the cup of tea waiting at home. You had to find a chair and say, "Of course, sit down. Let's have a talk."

If you can help a child to solve a problem, whether it's a big problem or a little one, if you can help a child to find the exact Guide Law that applies to her problem, if you can help her to see that Guiding isn't just a once a week fun session but something she must learn to live all the time, every minute of the day, then you are a Guider! I know that being a Guider isn't easy. The late King George VI found that being a king wasn't an easy job. In his Christmas broadcast to the Commonwealth in 1939 he quoted some lines of Minnie Louise Haskins, lines that he liked and found helpful:

> And I said to the man who stood at
> the gate of the year: "Give me a light
> that I may tread safely into the
> unknown." And he replied: "Go out
> into the darkness and put your hand
> into the hand of God. That shall
> be to you better than light and
> safer than a known way."

I want to thank everyone here today, and all those who cannot be here, for carrying the torch that I and thousands like me lit over sixty years ago. If you can pass to your girls the inner meaning and spirit of Guiding as the old Chief envisaged it, then I know the torch will never be extinguished.

The 5th New Barnet (Lyonsdown) **Guide Company**
invite you to come

and sample their

GUIDE PIE

ON

Saturday, 19th February 1938

in the

Lyonsdown Church Hall,

at 7.30 p.m.

The Ingredients used are to Suit all Tastes.

Doors open 7 p.m.

Prices per portion are 2/-, and 1/-
- to be paid for in advance. -

These can be obtained from any Member of the Company or from
the Caretaker at the Hall.

Guides and Scouts in Uniform 1/- and 9d
per portion.

Morgan, Printer, 6 Plantagenet Road, New Barnet.

ACKNOWLEDGEMENTS

To Richard Moses, my friend and mentor, my heartfelt thanks for his support. Together we agreed that these memoirs deserved a wider audience than the family, and it was he who found FriesenPress. He came with me to some of our meetings, and his advice and opinion has been invaluable.

Thanks, too, to Elna Gravelle, proof-reader par excellence and computer wizard extraordinaire. Now you can read the whole book, Elna!

Astra Crompton at FriesenPress, Thank you for your efficiency and patience.

And now, my sister Mary. While managing her life as a professor at the University of British Columbia in the Faculty of Education, and writing books of her own, she found time to organize my mother's memoirs and write the excellent introductions to each chapter. Mary died in January, 2009. I hope she would approve of what I have done.

And, finally, what can I say of my mother, Nesta. I have learned so much about her from these memoirs. I was an 'afterthought' in the family and, due to her war service in the Second World War, I saw much less of her in the holidays from boarding school than most of my friends did of their mothers. But I always knew she was a strong woman who had led a full life. It was not until I read these memoirs that I knew just how full it was. I am immensely proud to be her daughter.

Margaret Spencer
Salt Spring Island, B.C.
2015

Printed in Canada